WHi Image ID 27465

# Odd Wisconsin

## Amusing, Perplexing, and Unlikely Stories from Wisconsin's Past

*erika janik*

Wisconsin Historical Society Press

Published by the Wisconsin Historical Society Press
*Publishers since 1855*

## wisconsinhistory.org

Printed in the United States
Cover and text designed by Timothy O'Keeffe

11 10 09    2 3 4 5

On the front cover: Girl band with cows. WHi Image ID 2115

Library of Congress Cataloging-in-Publication Data

Janik, Erika.
Odd Wisconsin : amusing, perplexing, and unlikely stories from
Wisconsin's past / Erika Janik.
p. cm.
Includes index.
ISBN 978-0-87020-383-1 (pbk. : alk. paper)  1. Wisconsin—History—
Anecdotes. 2. Curiosities and wonders—Wisconsin—Anecdotes. 3. Wisconsin
—Biography—Anecdotes.  I. Title.
F581.6.J36 2007
977.5—dc22

                    2007011299

∞ The paper used in this publication meets the minimum requirements of the American National Standard for Information Sciences—Permanence of Paper for Printed Library Materials, ANSI Z39.48–1992.

*To my dad, who loved Wisconsin first.*

# Contents

# *Acknowledgments*

If the reader finds this history entertaining, enlightening, or surprising, then it is because Michael Edmonds, deputy director of the
Library-Archives at the Wisconsin Historical Society, came up with
the idea and made it a reality. So it is him that I thank for this odd
and playful take on Wisconsin history and for his belief in me to
pull it all together. I am indebted to the past librarians and archivists
at the Wisconsin Historical Society who had the foresight to think
that even oddity was worthy of collection alongside more scholarly
and notable tomes on state history, and to the many WHS Press
editors who for more than 150 years have researched and documented the state's history. *Odd Wisconsin* would be lost without the
hundreds of newspaper articles in the "Wisconsin Local History and
Biography Articles" database, the Wisconsin Historical Collections,
and the fabulous documents in the Society archives. I thank the
Wisconsin Historical Society Press, particularly Kathy Borkowski
and Kate Thompson, for thinking that *Odd Wisconsin* would make
a good book and for entrusting it to my care. Finally, I thank my
parents, Bill and Karin, for putting up with me and my whims, historical or otherwise.

# Introduction

If it's the offbeat, the paranormal, or the downright odd that you crave, there may be no better place than Wisconsin. Wisconsin's past is full of crazy characters, bizarre events, and surprising incidents that somehow didn't make the official account of state history—and the state would not be the same without them. Wisconsin's published history often seems less a story of real people than a prepackaged "virtual reality," neatly grouped by decade and offering the big speeches, the big names, and the big moments. Let's face it—these stories are a lot less fun.

Despite this, history has always been one of my favorite subjects because I had teachers who read between the lines. I loved hearing stories about where we came from and why. Family trips were usually educational: my parents thought it equally important to visit George Washington's Mount Vernon as it was to see Francis Johnson's huge ball of twine in Darwin, Minnesota. I was blessed with teachers who thought it was important to make history three-dimensional by sharing the stories that slipped through the cracks of our textbooks—and hearing those stories felt like getting inside information. History is more than a list of names and dates, and it isn't a smooth ride to the present day. *Odd Wisconsin* offers Wisconsin with all the bumps, bruises, and perplexities that make a place more than a location on a map or an entry in an encyclopedia.

While "Fighting Bob" La Follette's exploits as a leader in the Progressive Era are legendary, did you know that he personally saved countless valuable government documents and executive department paintings from destruction during the capitol fire of 1904? Or that the practice of placing Bibles in hotel and motel rooms originated in a Boscobel hotel more than one hundred years ago? Lowering the bucket into the well of history brings to light some of these curious fragments of Wisconsin's past. Some are simply amusing or unexpected—that happened here? Others are completely strange and creepy. But all contain some truth and have a historical point. These stories present an important and intrinsic part of Wisconsin's past and are worthy of recognition. One thing is certain: while the accuracy of some might not hold up under intense scrutiny, all of the tales contained here reflect real people, real events, and real reporting from the time.

*Odd Wisconsin* is your history, my history, our history—and it is a history in which we can take a kind of quirky pride, because it is hard to believe that any state could be odder than Wisconsin.

# I
# Odd Lives
# & Strange Deaths

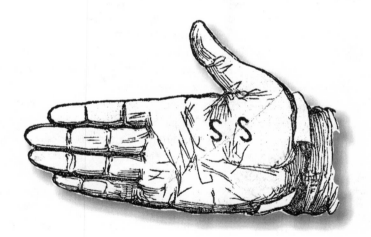

# 1918:
## Mob Rule Crushes Conscience

On September 14, 1918, two hundred people surrounded the Clark County home of Mrs. Caroline Krueger because her three sons refused to serve in the First World War. "They said that if the war was in this country they would be among the first to volunteer," reported a neighbor. "They declared however that it was not right to send American soldiers to France and that they never would go."

The family was known for its religious and pacifist views, but that didn't restrain a mob of patriotic citizens. When the boys refused to respond to their draft notices, deputies tried to arrest them, and a shoot-out followed in the Krueger family cornfield. A mob soon assembled outside the Krueger home, peppering the house with hundreds of bullets in an attempt to force the boys into the army. One of the sons, Frank, was shot through both legs and a member of the mob killed before a flag of truce persuaded Mrs. Krueger and her injured son to surrender. Mrs. Krueger's other two sons, Leslie and Ennis, managed to escape. When officials entered the farmhouse after the violence, they found an American flag mounted above the hearth. Leslie was later captured in

Minnesota, charged, and convicted for murder along with his mother and Frank.

Ennis was supposedly killed by a posse who found him sleeping in a nearby haystack a few days after the skirmish. Mrs. Krueger, however, thought otherwise. For years after the shoot-out, Mrs. Krueger refused to believe that the man in the haystack was her son Ennis, despite the death certificate. She claimed to have received letters from him and that others had seen and talked to him. She even had the body exhumed and refused to mark his grave or recognize the body as that of her son. No one knows for certain what happened to Ennis Krueger.

*Photo collage of the Krueger family of Clark County, who refused to serve in WWI.*

*Milwaukee Journal*, September 17, 1918

# *The Dodgeville Hermit*

*Archibald McArthur, the Dodgeville Hermit.*

*Milwaukee Journal*, January 31, 1926

*A* century ago, Archibald McArthur (1844–1925) was a celebrity of sorts. He arrived in Dodgeville just after the Civil War without a penny but soon became a successful young attorney, amassing a fortune in the process. He dressed in the latest fashions, owned the finest horse in town, started a newspaper, and became a mortgage lender to the citizens.

Then one day in middle age, he had a change of heart. McArthur gave away his finery, sold off his newspaper, refused to practice law, grew a beard, became a vegetarian, and entered into a hermit's life in his home on Main Street. He took a private vow of poverty, shunned alcohol and tobacco, and dressed in tattered overalls. He spent much of his time in the village cemetery, where he claimed to be able to communicate with spirits. He kept to himself: everyone knew who he was, but no one really knew him.

In 1922, at age seventy-eight, he abruptly bought an automobile, loaded his few possessions in it, and drove himself to Florida to live out his remaining years. By then he was worth more than a quarter of a million dollars (about three million dollars today). When he revised his will, he left each of his surviving relatives only five dollars—and gave nearly all the rest of his fortune to a stranger who once befriended him on a park bench.

McArthur never married, left no children, appeared to have no close friends, and never explained his motives or his actions in writing. He simply lives on in Wisconsin history as the "Dodgeville Hermit."

# *He Weighed 450 Pounds, Too*

*D*ateline: Mineral Point, Wisconsin, 1840. A famous character in early Mineral Point, the "Scotch Giant" Randall was known throughout the lead region for his "conspicuous" size and strength. Frederick Chadwick Randall could twirl a plow over his head like a club and carry a dozen eggs in one hand. At times, Randall traveled with the circus, although his main occupation was as a teamster. But it's his mammoth shoes that have come down through history. A man named Mark W. Terrill donated to the Wisconsin Historical Society the foot-shaped form on which Randall's giant shoes were sewn. Measuring thirteen and a half inches long and almost four inches wide, the shoes are only an inch shorter than Shaquille O'Neal's size 22 Reeboks.

*The shoe form used to measure the Scotch Giant's footwear, thirteen and a half inches long.*

Wisconsin Historical Museum Item #1968.15.1; photographed by Andrea Hoffman

# The Horror of Sauk County

*Y*ou thought Stephen King and Anne Rice invented American horror stories? Think again. Before they were even born, Wisconsin native son August Derleth (1909–1971) had started the publishing firm Arkham House to bring the weird, macabre, and fantastic

*August Derleth, Sauk City's storyteller, circa 1965.*

WHi Image ID 45660

to thousands of readers. Derleth published his first fiction in the magazine *Weird Tales* at age sixteen, and as an undergrad at UW–Madison in the 1920s he honed his craft under the guidance of Professor Helen C. White.

During the 1930s he published several books a year, befriended and published the science fiction writer H.P. Lovecraft, and became one of Wisconsin's most successful and prolific writers. In his hometown of Sauk City, he built a modernist house with a thatch roof made of marsh grass from India to house his comic book collection and his personal library of twelve thousand books. Derleth was literary editor of Madison's *Capital Times* newspaper from 1941 to 1960 and continued to write several books a year until his death. These included detective stories, volumes of poetry, histories, biographies, juvenile books about the Badger State, his own journals, and the multivolume *Sauk Prairie Saga* about his native town, as well as the Wisconsin volume in the Works Progress Administration's Rivers of America series. He even set a horror story among the Wisconsin Historical Society's old basement newspaper stacks, where a researcher who is accidentally locked in when the building closes goes insane from being surrounded by thousands of articles about murder, violence, mayhem, and death (no one's ever actually been locked in overnight—so far as we know).

By the mid-1960s Derleth had published upward of three thousand individual articles and stories and ninety books. Today, his first editions fetch up to seven thousand dollars each, and he retains a cult following among science fiction and fantasy readers.

# Jefferson's Black Descendants in Wisconsin

*R*umors that Thomas Jefferson fathered children with a slave, Sally Hemings, started more than two hundred years ago with a September 1802 article in a Richmond, Virginia, newspaper. According to a 2000 article in *Nature*, DNA analysis has proven to the satisfaction of leading historians that Jefferson was indeed the likely father of Eston Hemings (1808–1856), who moved to Wisconsin in 1852 with his wife and three children. A cabinetmaker and musician, Eston Hemings (who added Jefferson to his name when he moved to Wisconsin) died soon after coming to Madison and left little evidence of himself in the public record.

Eston's eldest child was John W. Jefferson (1835–1892), proprietor in the late 1850s of Madison's American House hotel, across North Pinckney street from the state capitol. He led Wisconsin's Eighth Infantry during the Civil War and sent letters home to the press. After being wounded twice, Colonel Jefferson was mustered out in October 1864. Eston Hemings Jefferson's second child was a daughter named Anna W. Jefferson (1836–1866).

*Beverly Jefferson, the likely grandson of Thomas Jefferson and Sally Hemings.*

WHi Image ID 35742

She married in Madison but died young and, like her father, left few traces of herself in local documents. Eston's youngest child, Beverly Jefferson (1839–1908), worked for his brother and served briefly in the war before himself becoming proprietor of the American House and later, in the 1860s, of the Capitol House hotel. As a prominent hotel keeper in Madison and operator of a carriage and trucking service, he was well known to most of the state's late-nineteenth-century political leaders and was thought of as having a "cordial word for every soul." All of these grandchildren of Sally Hemings and Thomas Jefferson had light complexions like their grandmother and passed as white in census and other public records. The entire Eston Hemings family is buried in Forest Hill Cemetery in Madison.

## Large Living

*F*rederick and Jane Shadick may have been Wisconsin's biggest residents—and certainly its biggest couple.

From 1849 to 1854 they lived in a stone house at Cottage Inn, near Belmont in Lafayette County, where they farmed and worked in a pottery factory. Fred also drove teams of oxen hauling lead between Helena and Galena, Illinois. He was seven feet four inches tall and weighed 450 pounds; Jane was also over seven feet tall. Fred could pick up an eighty-pound chunk of lead with one hand, carry fence rails like other people carry fishing poles, and lift a full four hundred–pound whiskey barrel with his fingertips.

Once, when they needed a dozen eggs, Fred was asked how he'd carry them home. "Guess I can get 'em all in here," he replied, cupping the palm of his hand. His shoes were four inches wide and thirteen and a half inches long. Often subject to public ridicule, the Shadicks spent their free time in the fall, winter, and spring alone together, filling their stone cottage with books.

But each summer, public ridicule worked to their advantage, when they supplemented their income traveling as a circus sideshow, Fred under the stage name "the Scotch Giant." They knew the routine because when they first arrived in America, they'd been exhibited by P.T. Barnum alongside General Tom Thumb as "Mr. & Mrs. Randell, Giants." On July 4, 1854, Fred died of a stroke while on tour in Indiana with Franconi's Hippodrome Circus, and Jane died a few months later. Their enormous frames were laid to rest side by side in the village of Rewey, in Iowa County. (Making an odd story odder: could Frederick Shadick also have been known as Frederick Chadwick Randall, the "Scotch Giant" [see page 6]? Despite discrepancies in the historical record, similar details suggest they were one and the same.)

# Lee Harvey Oswald of April 1865

When Abraham Lincoln was gunned down on the night of April 14, 1865, John Wilkes Booth was seen fleeing Ford's Theatre by W. D. Kenzie of Beloit, who heard gunshots and saw the actor-assassin leap from the balcony and get away. Another Wisconsin man, W. H. De Groff, was outside the theater and saw Booth escape on horseback.

Kenzie was acquainted with Booth and knew him well on sight, so he quickly joined the soldiers who pursued the murderer into Virginia where Booth was killed twelve days later. Called over to identify the body, Kenzie knelt on the ground to take a look. "That's not Booth. This fellow's a red headed Virginian, I said." Kenzie claimed to have been told to keep quiet by his superiors. Kenzie always believed that it was not Booth but rather an imposter who was shot that day and that Booth escaped alive in an elaborate cover-up to appease public clamor for justice.

He was not alone in thinking this. This theory, like Kennedy assassination conspiracy theories, persisted for decades and spawned a series of books and articles. Modern historians, however, with access to volumes of forensic and archival evidence, disagree and have no doubt that Booth met his end in the Virginia barn described by historians ever since.

# Looking Down
# on the Competition

*The grave of Michel Brisbois, high above Prairie du Chien.*

WHi Image ID 45761

14

*A*ccording to local legend, fur trader Michel Brisbois (1759–1837) had himself interred high on a bluff over Prairie du Chien so he could forever look down on his rivals.

Brisbois was an independent trader who arrived in Wisconsin in 1781. For the next forty years he paid little attention to the wishes of the authorities, undercutting more prosperous traders and even selling goods to both sides during the War of 1812 (he was later accused of treason but was acquitted). Brisbois went head-to-head with well-connected and affluent merchants such as Joseph Rolette and Hercules Dousman, both of whom were agents for the American Fur Company. In 1818, Rolette upped the ante by marrying Jane Fisher, whom Brisbois and his wife had raised in their home.

Brisbois continued to disregard convention for the rest of his career. As he approached death, the legend says, he bought a hilltop parcel overlooking Prairie du Chien so that his rivals would know he was looking down on them from the grave. He was buried high on that bluff in 1837.

Brisbois's adopted daughter Jane may have had the last laugh. About the time that Brisbois died, she separated from Rolette, insisting he build her a house as part of their separation agreement. Shortly afterward Rolette was ruined by John Jacob Astor, and he died in poverty in 1842. Jane promptly married Brisbois's other rival, Dousman, and became mistress of the finest fur trade mansion in the West, Villa Louis. Both houses now belong to the Wisconsin Historical Society and are open to the public, with Michel Brisbois looking down on them from his final resting place high above.

# The Man with the Branded Hand

*"With that front of calm endurance,
on whose steady nerve in vain, Pressed the iron of the prison,
smote the fiery shafts of pain . . ."*

—John Greenleaf Whittier in *Voices of Freedom* (1846)

$\mathcal{S}$oon after Whittier wrote those lines, the man with the branded hand moved to Wisconsin. He was Captain Jonathan Walker, who retired to Fond du Lac and, later, Washington County after five years spent lecturing and writing against slavery. He had a uniquely grisly device for making his point from the lecture stage—the palm of his right hand had been branded by a Florida court with the letters "S.S." for "slave stealer."

In 1844 Walker, a middle-aged Massachusetts sea captain on business in the Caribbean, attempted to carry several fugitive slaves from Pensacola, Florida, to the British West Indies, where slavery was illegal. His boat, however, was seized and brought to the authorities at Key West, where Walker was charged with theft of the slave owner's "property." He was sent back to Pensacola and, after a long confinement in a Florida prison, was sentenced to pay a large fine and to have his right hand branded.

"When about to be branded," Walker wrote afterward in his book *Trial and Imprisonment of Jonathan Walker*, "I was placed in the prisoner's box. [The court officer] proceeded to tie my hand to

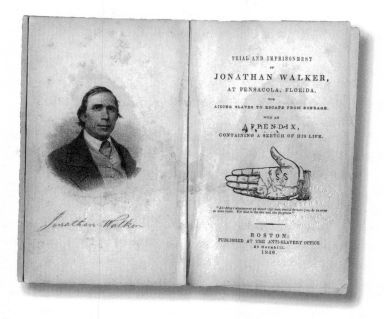

*Frontspiece and title page from Jonathan Walker's book* The Trial and Imprisonment of Jonathan Walker, *published in 1846.*

a part of the railing in front. I remarked that there was no need of tying it, for I would hold still. He observed that it was best to make sure, and tied it firmly to the post, in fair view; he then took from the fire the branding-iron, of a slight red heat, and applied it to the ball of my hand, and pressed it on firmly, for fifteen or twenty seconds. It made a spattering noise, like a handful of salt in the fire, as the skin seared and gave way to the hot iron. The pain was severe while the iron was on, and for some time afterwards."

Walker is said to have tolerated this pain stoically, knowing it was no worse than that which his compatriots in the ship and their families were likely to undergo, or that African Americans commonly suffered at the hands of slave owners.

After his release from prison, Walker became a celebrity of sorts, and from 1845 to 1849 he lectured on the antislavery circuit in the company of fugitive slave Henry Watson. He also wrote books and pamphlets about his experience and in support of abolition. His treatment shocked and outraged citizens across the country and helped to crystallize in the public mind the brutalizing effects that slave owning caused on the human soul. It helped raise public consciousness about the issue years before the Fugitive Slave Act, Dred Scott, or *Uncle Tom's Cabin* had made slavery a universally discussed institution.

Walker retired from the limelight by moving with his large family to Wisconsin in 1851, living here throughout the great fugitive slave controversies and the entire Civil War. In 1866 he moved to Lake Harbor, Michigan, where he operated a small fruit orchard until his death in 1878; some of his descendants stayed on in Wisconsin. He liked to say that the letters burned into his flesh actually stood for "Slave Saver."

## Mohawk Indian or French Prince?

$\mathcal{E}$leazer Williams is surely one of the oddest characters in Wisconsin history. Born and raised among the Mohawk Indians, Williams was sent as a teenager to the missionary school that would evolve into Dartmouth College. He became a Protestant missionary himself, and his intelligence and eloquence gave him entry into both Indian and white communities.

When he was in his thirties, Williams used these skills to help the Oneida and other nations who were rapidly being dispossessed of their lands in the East. At the instigation of the U.S. government, Williams and tribal leaders explored opportunities for a new home-land in the West for the Stockbridge, Munsee, Brotherton, Oneida, and other Christian Indians of New York and New England. In 1820 he led a delegation of them to Wisconsin to negotiate with the Menominee for territory around Green Bay where they could take refuge from Eastern land speculators. These negotiations dragged on for more than a decade. While they were still under way, in 1823, Williams married a fourteen-year-old Menominee-French girl named Marie Madeline Jourdain, perhaps to gain influence with his negotiating partners (according to her descendants, the marriage was short-lived).

Albert Ellis, another Indian advocate, reported that Williams envisioned a great nation of Christian Indians growing

*Portrait of the "Lost Dauphin," Eleazer Williams.*

*Eleazer Williams*, by George Catlin, circa 1833; Wisconsin Historical Museum #1942.156; WHi Image ID 3021

20

up in the West with himself as their ruler. The Oneida and other so-called New York Indians had other ideas, however, and when negotiations with the Menominee were finally completed, they repudiated his leadership and sent him packing. With his dream of ruling an Indian empire shattered, Williams became a roving missionary supported by Indian communities and white religious organizations in Wisconsin and New York.

But in middle age he came up with another way to be an emperor: he began to claim that he was the long-lost child of Louis XVI and Marie Antoinette who had been spirited away to America for safekeeping when they were beheaded during the French Revolution. Though his friends laughed at the idea, Williams convinced some European aristocrats he was heir to the French throne—enough to create a stream of transatlantic donations that helped support him in his final years. He even tricked his mother into swearing he'd been adopted and began issuing manifestos and signing letters "Louis, Dauphin." Ellis, who had known him since childhood, called Williams "the most perfect adept at fraud, deceit, and intrigue that the world ever produced."

When he died in 1858, Williams's last words were about a dress in his possession having been worn by Marie Antoinette. DNA tests recently confirmed Williams's deceit, proving that the real dauphin had indeed died in 1795.

# Our Own Indiana Jones

*Explorer Roy Chapman Andrews with his wife, Billie,
at their Connecticut country home.*

Back cover of Roy Chapman Andrews's *An Explorer Comes Home*. (New York:
Doubleday, 1947.) Available at the Wisconsin Historical Society Library.

*T*rotting the globe in search of adventure, Roy Chapman Andrews suffered blistering sandstorms, fended off deadly snakes, and escaped roving bandits to become a world-famous fossil hunter.

Raised in Beloit, Andrews once said, "I was born to be an explorer" and, like so many other famous sons and daughters of Wisconsin, he left the Badger State as soon as he possibly could. After graduating from Beloit College, he landed in New York in 1906, using money saved from his job as a taxidermist. He applied for a position at the American Museum of Natural History but was told that no jobs were available. Ever persistent, Andrews asked if he could scrub the museum floors and was given a job. Over the next thirty years, his scientific expeditions carried him from New York to Indonesia, China, and Central Asia, usually with a cowboy hat and a revolver. The press portrayed him as a swashbuckling scientist who conquered the Gobi Desert and Mongolia to discover dinosaurs and recover relics. He did, in fact, survive life-threatening encounters with armed bandits, deadly pythons, angry whales, and hungry sharks and was erroneously reported dead more than once as he roamed the world in the name of science.

Andrews is widely believed to have been a model for the movie legend Indiana Jones (made famous by actor Harrison Ford), although, according to the Virtual Exploration Society, producer George Lucas never specifically cited Andrews as the inspiration for that character. "However," the Society's biography of Andrews states, "in 1977 he did tell Steven Spielberg when they first discussed the concept for the movie trilogy that he had been inspired by movie serials he had seen in the 1940's and the 1950's. It is likely that the writers for those films, in turn, had been inspired by the real-life adventures of explorers like Andrews from a generation before. Although Andrews was the most high profile of these explorers it is possible that other figures, like Percy Fawcett and W. Douglas Burden also contributed to the archetype of the dashing adventurer/scientist that appeared in those Saturday afternoon B flicks that Lucas enjoyed as a kid."

From 1934 to 1942 Andrews served as the director of the Natural History Museum, but after a life of adventure he probably didn't much enjoy the staid institutional halls. He moved to California in 1942 and spent the rest of his life writing about his experiences. He described his many expeditions in several books, including *Meet Your Ancestors* (1945), *In the Days of the Dinosaur* (1959), and the autobiographical works *Under a Lucky Star* (1943) and *An Explorer Comes Home* (1947). His popular books for lay audiences helped spawn a fascination for dinosaurs among children that shows no signs of waning fifty years later. Andrews died in Carmel, California, on March 11, 1960.

# A Paranoid Was After Him

*O*n a March evening in 1872, Dr. John Garner of Milwaukee had a vivid premonition of his impending murder. An hour later, Garner was shot dead when he opened his front door; his assailant flew off into the night. The murderer, Sarah Josephine Wilner, had traveled all the way from Ashtabula, Ohio, to Garner's doorstep, arriving at the Milwaukee depot at the very same time that the doctor's fears were most pronounced. "I never had such a feeling in all my life," Garner had remarked to his brother-in-law. "I feel as if something were closing in on me, trying to crush me." His fears were, unfortunately, soon realized.

Wilner, a onetime patient of Garner's, had gone mad after the death of her husband and two children and believed herself afflicted with "medical odors" projected toward her by a league of Milwaukee doctors intent on her ruin. While she held various Milwaukee doctors responsible, she focused on Garner, who had been her most frequent physician. Declared insane, Wilner spent the rest of her life in an asylum in Wauwatosa, and poor Dr. Garner's psychic disturbance became the stuff of legend.

*Retail Giant*

*H. Gordon Selfridge, department store innovator.*

WHi Image ID 45848

Ripon native H. Gordon Selfridge worked his way up through Marshall Field and Company and took his Midwest American optimism into the heart of the staid British Empire, reimagining the modern department store in the process. "I was pretty much the wild and untamed man from the wild and untamed west when I came to London from Chicago," recounted Selfridge years later in the *Milwaukee Journal* on September 9, 1932. Astonished at the unattractive displays and "obsequious condescension" of employees in London shops, Selfridge decided to show them a thing or two. In 1909 he opened his own American-style department store, Selfridges, on London's Oxford Street.

Selfridge was one of the first retailers to appreciate the psychology of shopping. He covered his store's floors with comfortable carpets and welcomed browsers who bought nothing but just wanted to "make a day of it" (as he phrased it in his advertising). He constructed lounges, restaurants, and tearooms for rest between rounds of shopping, as well as a roof garden with views of the city. He was also among the first to realize that women were the principal consumers in most households, and so he emphasized cosmetics, beauty products, and carefully crafted window displays meant to appeal to them.

Toward the end of his career, he returned home to receive an honorary degree from Ripon College.

# Spurned Inventor
## Creates Suicide Machine

Dateline: Kenosha, Wisconsin, 1930. Denied credit, profit, riches, rest, or peace, a neglected inventor employed his professional skills to make a dramatic exit from his vale of tears. Howard E. Harbaugh had moved to Kenosha from Illinois in 1892 and quickly put his aptitude for machinery to work for local industries. Among his inventions was the first automatic circle knitting machine used in many knitting mills and a machine that wove wire springs for mattresses. Harbaugh also worked as a contract-inventor for the Chicago-Rockford Hosiery Company. Retiring with no fame or wealth to his name, Harbaugh had become an eccentric character, often seen doddering around town with cane in hand and spectacles slipping down his nose.

In the end, Harbaugh used his "splendid genius for destruction" on himself, placing a 12-gauge shotgun in a vice and attaching a slender strap to the trigger. He ran the strap backward and upward over an awl driven into the wall to create a direct pull and pulled the trigger.

# Wisconsin's First Poet

*P*oet and scientist James Gates Percival was one of early Wisconsin's most learned men but also one of its most eccentric. Utterly lacking in ambition and confidence, the outcast scholar mastered a dozen languages and the emerging science of geology while huddled in seclusion among his books and herbarium. Before moving to Wisconsin, Percival lived, like a storybook character, in a garret, writing poetry and becoming a hack writer for distinguished literary men. Some even claimed—falsely—that Percival was the sole author, compiler, and editor of the first edition of Noah Webster's dictionary.

According to the August 15, 1920, *Madison Democrat*, in 1853 Percival came to Wisconsin and traveled around the state in a "tattered gray coat with trousers patched by himself, and an old weather-beaten glazed cap, ear-pieces of sheepskin." Named Wisconsin's first state geologist in middle age, he spent his days crouched in holes and caves and returned home "with weary knees to a supperless cottage to feast on moonshine."

29

*James Gates Percival, eccentric poet and scientist.*

WHi Image ID 45760

# II
## Curiosities

# Buying the Farm

"Buying the farm" took on a literal meaning in the early twentieth century when banker and land developer Benjamin Faast organized the Wisconsin Colonization Company in northern Wisconsin. In 1917 Faast purchased about fifty thousand acres of land in Sawyer County. He divided the land into farm sites and began to offer them ready-equipped to immigrant farmers. Although not Faast's first development scheme for northern Wisconsin, his plans for Sawyer County were scaled to a whole new level of magnitude—both in amenities offered to settlers and in his vision for the future.

Promotional literature promised that each farm came with land, an "attractive house and barn, a cow, 2 pigs and 6 chickens, a set of clearing tools and clover and timothy seed." Houses came in four styles and were "attractively painted in striking contrast with the average tar paper shack and log cabin of the pioneer." Beautifying the town and home sites was of the utmost importance to Faast, who believed that the happiness of the townspeople was directly tied to its aesthetic beauty. By providing seeds and garden plans, Faast encouraged settlers to contribute to the overall appearance of the community with flowers and vegetable gardens.

The farm sites were only the beginning of Faast's grand vision—he also mapped out what he hoped would become the centerpiece of the colony, a prosperous city he named Ojibwa, "the first planned and carefully thought out rural town in the whole Chippewa Valley, if not in all Wisconsin." The plan for Ojibwa included a zoo, parks, streets with sidewalks, a restaurant, a large general store, and neighborhoods that took "advantage of the natural beauty spots."

Unfortunately, Faast's dream began to bottom out soon after it began, and the Wisconsin Colonization Company went bankrupt in 1929.

*Benjamin Faast drew settlers north with his made-to-order farms.*

Made-to-order farms / Wisconsin Colonization Co., Western Sales Office.
(Minneapolis: The Company, Western Sales Office, 1921[?].)
WHS Pamphlet Collection, PAM 56–3042

# English Tudor Logging Camp

*M*ost Northwoods villages began life near logging camps, with a few single-story, false-front frame buildings that housed a general store, a blacksmith, a post office, and a tavern—an entire village vaguely resembling the set of a Hollywood Western. There was a predictable sameness about "the ugly square front shops which seem to be the favorite style of architecture of the small town business men" and the "dingy boarding houses or patched huts of tar paper" that housed the village residents, as one traveler wrote.

But not at Elcho, in Langlade County. According to an account in the March 14, 1924, *Door County Advocate*, a fire destroyed the village in 1923, but rather than see this as a great calamity, mill owner Charles W. Fish decided it was an opportunity to rebuild in the "most desirable and idealistic manner possible." Instead of throwing up the same types of boring and ugly structures that had been destroyed, he hired a Chicago architect to make the main street look like a traditional English village. This was such a remarkable sight amid the endless bogs, acres of stumps, and desolate burnt forests of the north that when trains approached the village, passengers would "shout to each other and all make haste to the right side of the car."

Half-timber Tudor-style structures stood alongside one another on Main Street, "each in turn marked by its own charm but all conforming to the same idea of beauty. . . . Although the eye passes from one to another, it is impossible to decide which is the most pleasing." One visitor remarked, "If I had seen such a business street in England or France I would have said: Yes, such a village of beauty is possible in an ancient well ordered land of culture. But to find such a paragon in the wilderness of Northern Wisconsin, that is impossible. I pinch myself in the arm and stare out with my face to the window-pane until the train is again engulfed in the ravaged wilderness."

*Elcho's Muskie Inn, built according to Charles Fish's English Tudor–style vision.*

WHi Image ID 45658

# Finally! Relief from Those Embarrassing Holes...

*L*ong before the advent of nylon pantyhose in 1938, Milwaukee's own Holeproof Hosiery was producing high-quality, light, and durable silk-blend hosiery for fashionable women and men. Company founder Carl Freschl took hosiery to high art, experimenting for years before hitting upon just the right blend of fibers and intricate knitting technique to make "Holeproof a household word throughout the world" (according to the company's advertising brochure). Holeproof Hosiery produced a variety of styles for men, women, and children in different silk blends and colors that were available "in every civilized county on the globe." The company name said it all, and it was backed up by a six-month hole-free guarantee. Today, when bare legs seem to be the order of the day, let Holeproof remind you that hosiery is "always in good taste."

*Holeproof Hosiery steaming and drying on foot-shaped metal forms.*

*Better Hosiery: The story of Holeproof.* (Milwaukee, Wis.: Holeproof Hosiery Company, 1924.) WHS Pamphlet Collection, PAM 57–555

37

# Gardener Grows Seat from Seed

"I watched and assisted nature in growing a piece of furniture," explained John Krusback, president of Shawano County's Embarrass State Bank. A gardener as well as a banker, Krusback was inspired to grow a chair in 1903.

Krusback started by germinating and nurturing thirty-two box elder seeds into healthy sprouts. Four years later he transplanted the young trees into a chair-sized spot in his yard. "I left them to grow in their new home for a year until they were six feet tall," he told a reporter. In the spring of 1908 he "began the work of training the young and pliable stems to grow gradually in the shape of a chair bending the stems of these trees and tying and grafting them together so as to grow, if possible, with all joints cemented by nature."

With the saplings bent and tied, nature ran its course. The frame grew securely together, and over the next four years, Krusback shaped shoots and branches into the seat, arms, and back. By 1912 only the four legs actually grew from roots—the rest of the botanical chair sprouted from the grafts he had carefully attached. Finally, in 1914, after eleven years of cultivation, Krusback cut the legs off at ground level and moved the chair inside, where the *Shawano Leader* newspaper hailed it the country's "only natural grown chair."

# The Kaukauna Gold Rush of 1900

The desire to get rich quick is an inextinguishable little flame burning in the core of too many human hearts. Whether it's slot machines, the lottery, the California gold rush, or the Great Lakes fur trade, there never seems to be a shortage of people willing to jump on board and try to get something for nothing—which is what they usually get. The March 18, 1919, *Manitowoc Herald* reported that, around 1900, when Alaska's Klondike gold rush was in the news, two Lawrence College students duped their neighbors into believing that gold was discovered near Kaukauna. After all, if it could happen in Alaska, why not Kaukauna?

A young, roughly dressed man had strolled into a saloon carrying a sparkling gold rock and declared that, young as he was, he had hunted gold in the wilds of Canada, and he knew ore when he saw it. The man planned to go to Appleton to have it assayed. News of the find spread quickly, and a rush of men who expected to be rich descended on Appleton to have their brilliant, glistening rocks tested. There being no assayer in town, a young Lawrence College chemist agreed to test the specimens for a fee. The young student was at least honest with the men, informing them that they had in fact found iron pyrites—fool's gold. Embarrassed, the men never told anyone that they had been lured by fool's gold. And at five dollars a person to perform their test, the two students made a tidy sum that aided materially in financing their education.

# "Let Them Eat Cake"

That's what Marie Antoinette, Queen of France, is often thought to have remarked when the condition of starving peasants was reported to her. History caught up with her by replying "Off with her head," and she died under the guillotine at noon on October 16, 1793.

By then her wealth and palace had been plundered by the revolutionary mob. In one of history's oddities, her elaborately decorated mantel clock ended up in the Milwaukee home of Caroline Ogden, where it was keeping fine time 140 years after her execution.

After the sack of the Tuileries, the clock passed into the hands of the U.S. ambassador to France, Gouverneur Morris. Morris, an uncle of Ogden's grandfather, passed it down through the family until the splendid red marble clock landed in Milwaukee in the 1930s. Strangely enough, this was not the beheaded queen's only Wisconsin connection, as one of our state's most famous eccentrics, Eleazer Williams, actually claimed to be her son (see page 19).

*Marie Antoinette Clock Owned by Miss Caroline Ogden*

Gouverneur Morris Got the Timepiece After th
Tuilleries Was Sacked; It Was Inherited by His
Nephew, Miss Ogden's Grandfather.

By MARGE STANLEY.

*Marie Antoinette's clock, in the Milwaukee home of Caroline Ogden.*

*Milwaukee Sentinel*, December 3, 1933

41

# Madison: "Not Fit for Any Civilized Nation of People to Inhabit"

The first visitor to leave an account of the land that would become the city of Madison was Ebenezer Brigham, who passed through in May of 1829 while returning from Portage to his home in Blue Mounds. He later told an acquaintance: "The site was at the time an open prairie, on which grew dwarf oaks, while thickets covered the lower grounds. Struck with the strange beauty of the place, he predicted that a village or city would in time grow up there, and it might be the capital of a State."

Oddly enough, a few years later Jefferson Davis, who would lead the Confederate States of America during the Civil War, camped in the same place. Davis recalled in 1885, "While on detached service in the summer of 1829, I think I encamped one night about the site of Madison. The nearest Indian village was on the opposite side of the lake. . . . I and the file of soldiers who accompanied me were the first white men who ever passed over the country between the Portage . . . and the then village of Chicago. Fish and waterfowl were abundant; deer and pheasants less plentiful. The Indians subsisted largely on Indian corn and wild rice."

Madison's potential was not obvious to all early visitors, however. To the soldiers chasing Black Hawk in the summer of 1832, the future capital seemed unimpressive: "If these lakes were anywhere else except in the country they are," wrote one of them just after the war, "they would be considered among the wonders of the world. But the country they are situated in, is not fit for any civilized nation of people to inhabit."

Nevertheless, in September 1832, the U.S. government purchased from the Ho-Chunk land including the future site of Madison in a treaty signed at Rock Island. On December 4, 1834, U.S. government surveyor Orson Lyon began to run the township and section lines for Madison. Lyon found the future downtown "second rate [for farming, with] black, white & burr oak, red root grass & marsh, flags etc."

# Milwaukee to Madison and Beyond by Boat

Before Wisconsin was a state, some leading citizens of the town called Milwaukee suggested that a canal be dug between Lake Michigan and the Rock River near Fort Atkinson. The canal's proposed route would have passed roughly through Menomonee Falls, Pewaukee, Delafield, and Fort Atkinson, where it would have joined the Rock River, which in turn flowed down to the Mississippi at Rock Island. Lead from Mineral Point, New Diggings, Platteville, and other southwest Wisconsin towns would have floated down the Galena or Fever River and up the Rock, and then through the canal and the lakes of Waukesha County to Milwaukee. By damming the Yahara at the outlet of Lake Kegonsa near Stoughton, boats could also come up through the Four Lakes region to Madison, which was chosen to be the capital of Wisconsin in 1836.

Or so thought developer Byron Kilbourn and his chief of staff, Increase Lapham. They and their supporters petitioned the U.S. Congress for financial backing to get the project under way, and when that approach failed, they turned to the fledgling territorial legislature. With typical thoroughness and accuracy, Lapham documented the effort of the development company in his

*Documentary History of the Milwaukee and Rock River Canal*, compiled and published by order of the Board of Directors of the Milwaukee and Rock River Canal Company, issued in 1840.

Although the builders did complete 1.25 miles of canal on the west back of the Rock River, financial and technical difficulties delayed the project long enough for a new technology, the railroad, to make the canal unnecessary, and the project quietly slipped into oblivion.

*Naturalist and engineer Increase Lapham examines a meteorite, circa 1871.*

45

## Out of Whack

**W**hen Madison became a city in 1856, the area, marked by hundreds of effigy mounds, had already been populated by Native Americans for many centuries. Maybe that's why white settlers had trouble claiming it as their own.

In 1837 workers arrived to build the capitol. Surveyor Frank Hatheway was hired to lay out the Capitol Square, but when he tried to use his compass, an unknown force interfered with it. "Repeated trials made with the utmost care, on a north-and-south line," he recalled, "showed that lines run on the same course, as indicated by the needle, crossed each other at every attempt." This was not the first time that surveyors had been foiled in their efforts—surveyors from Brown County and Mineral Point had attempted to do the work but had abandoned it after repeated failures.

After a week of frustration, Hatheway was reporting his inability to make the survey to the commissioner when "it fortunately happened that a traveler who had stopped at our boarding house for the night, on his way across the country, heard our conversation; at its conclusion, he approached me, and, asking a few questions relative to the work in hand, suggested a mode of operation which at once seemed to remove all difficulties. It would take too much time and space to explain in detail the modus operandi; suffice it to say, that the plan recommended was adopted, and was entirely successful."

So did the traveler suggest a way to compensate for magnetic deviation, a way to pacify ancient spirits, or simply a way to make the streets look straight to the naked eye? Hatheway didn't say, and "the next morning, the traveler (whose name I did not learn) resumed his journey, and I never again saw him." Madison has struck observers as slightly out of whack ever since.

*This 1855 plat map of Madison shows the Capitol Square at center.*

WHi Image ID 23644

# Sheep's Heads, Petrified Frogs, and Other Curios

When Wisconsin and its Historical Society were still young, citizens eagerly donated objects to its "cabinet of antiquities," hoping to build a collection to rival that of older and more prestigious East Coast institutions. And as Historical Society officials gathered objects for the collection, they looked far beyond Wisconsin's borders. Here's a small selection of the items donated during the year 1875:

- *A three-dollar continental bill dated February 17, 1776, paid to John Ormsby of Vermont for revolutionary services, preserved and presented by his descendants*

- *A cone of sugar pine tree, very large size, from the Nevada Mountains, Mariposa County, fifty miles southwest of Yosemite Valley, from Mrs. Daniel Jackson, Evansville*

- *Head of a Rocky Mountain sheep with large heavy horns, from James M. Stoner, Colorado*

- *A small petrified frog taken from a boulder of sand rock, eight feet below the surface, in digging a cellar for Peter Young, Madison*

- *Two bottles of water, one from the Dead Sea the other from the River Jordan, from Dr. C. B. Chapman*

- *A pewter platter, part of the marriage portion of the bride Eunice Marshall when married to Captain Samuel Enos in December 1735 at Windsor, Connecticut—presented by her great-granddaughter, Mrs. E. D. Pardee, Madison*

- *A common wooden chair formerly the property of President Fillmore, one of a set with which he commenced housekeeping about 1826*

- *A copy of the* VICKSBURG DAILY CITIZEN *July 2, 1863, printed on wallpaper, from Henry Joy*

- *A specimen of bread made by the Pueblo Indians, from Geo. H. Pradt*

At the time, the state's historical museum was presided over by Isaac Lyon, who, according to the *Twenty-second Report, Wisconsin Historical Collections*, Volume 7, "at the venerable age of eighty-one, has for another year given his undivided attention to the care of the cabinet and its exhibition to visitors and strangers—always eliciting the warmest expressions for his kindness from those who visit that interesting department." It was then housed in the south wing of the second Madison capitol.

In 1875 the Society also received on deposit one of the largest and most valuable collections of archaeological objects then in existence. Frederick S. Perkins of Burlington, Racine County, donated more than 9,000 stone rollers, pestles, knives, scrapers, awls, pikes, spears, lances, and arrowheads, and 150 ancient copper tools, making the Society museum one of the most important archaeological research collections in the country. "The stone collection is simply wonderful," beamed Society director Lyman Draper, "while the copper one is confessedly unequalled in the country."

# Shocking Developments on the Home Front: Electrical Power Transforms Domestic Life

*This is the porch where in the breeze*

*My lady irons at her ease*

*When summer makes the kitchen hot—*

*The Iron stays warm, the ironer not.*

*Fatigue's to her a stranger quite,*

*She does her work and finds it light—*

*In the Electrical House that Jack Built.*

So begins a 1916 advertising brochure from Milwaukee Electric Railway and Light Co., published to show how electric appliances could transform home life. Written in verse to parody the well-known nursery rhyme about "The House That Jack Built," and illustrated with drawings like those in children's books of the period, it celebrates the convenience, comfort, and health enjoyed by users of electrical appliances. Pictured are an electric iron, a coffee maker, a heater, a vacuum cleaner, and a clothes washer, as well as electric lights.

Today it seems odd that a utility company would have to advertise to get new customers to use its services. Electricity is so ubiquitous we forget that it was once unavailable and that people had to be convinced that

*If you but engage the service wires*

*That bring the aide that never tires*

*But works and works*

*And never shirks*

*In the Electrical House that Jack Built.*

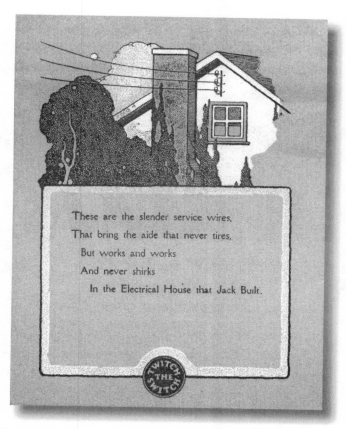

These are the slender service wires,

That bring the aide that never tires,

But works and works

And never shirks

In the Electrical House that Jack Built.

Milwaukee Electric Railway and Light Co. *The Electrical house that Jack built.* (Milwaukee, Wis.: Milwaukee Electric Railway and Light Co., 1916.) WHS Pamphlet Collection, PAM 57–580

*A Hillsboro and Northeastern Railroad locomotive, which carried passengers and groceries the 4.8 miles between Hillsboro and Union Center twice a day.*

WHi Image ID 45806

# Smallest Railroad in the World?

"Smallest railroad in the world" was the claim made by the not-so-mighty Hillsboro and Northeastern, which maintained a grand total of 4.8 miles of track between Hillsboro and Union Center, west of Wisconsin Dells. The *Wisconsin State Journal* of May 11, 1927, noted that, riding the rails, "the smoker would find his cigar about a third consumed and the woman would discover her conversation just beginning to gather momentum when the journey was finished." Built in 1902 by Edward Hammer Sr., the line was constructed in five days from local timber. Despite its short distance, the railroad was a success from day one, carrying passengers, livestock, butter, eggs, logs, lumber, and condensed milk on two round trips a day between Hillsboro and the Chicago & Northwestern line at Union Center.

# State's First Doctor a Black Woman

The first person paid to heal the sick in Wisconsin was a woman of color known as "Aunt Mary Ann" to her Prairie du Chien patients. Born of mixed parentage, Mary Ann Labuche came upriver about 1790 from near St. Louis, where African slaves had been brought in the 1720s. Married three times and the mother of fourteen children, she carried with her an esoteric knowledge of herbs, midwifery, and Indian and folk medicine that filled a crucial need on the Wisconsin frontier.

"She was," recalled her neighbor James Lockwood, "the only person pretending to a knowledge of the healing art. Until a fort was erected at Prairie du Chien [in 1816] and a surgeon arrived there with the troops, she was sent for by the sick and attended them as regularly as a physician, and charged fees therefor, giving them, as she expressed it, 'device and yarb drink.'" Aside from Labuche, the only other medical help was hundreds of miles away at Mackinac in Michigan.

"She was an excellent nurse," Lockwood continued, "and even after there were regular surgeons of the army stationed at Fort Crawford, Mary Ann continued to practice among the inhabitants" with such success that "we frequently joked to the physician about Mary Ann's superior skill in the healing art." Her talents were put to the test on June 26, 1827, when her baby granddaughter was scalped during an Indian attack. Labuche covered the exposed brain with a silver plate over which the skin healed, and the little girl lived eighty years.

# The Spy Who Died in the Dells

After the Civil War, Belle Boyd was as famous as any hot young celebrity is today. Boyd was a Virginia teenager when the war broke out, and her sympathies naturally lay with her homeland. Union troops soon occupied her town and tried to raise the stars and stripes over the Boyd family home. Her mother protested, and when one of the soldiers treated her rudely, seventeen-year-old Belle shot him dead.

Her beauty and . . . uhh, communication skills . . . allowed her to repeatedly gain the confidence of Union officers, whom she then successfully betrayed to the Confederates. She was more than once captured by federal troops and imprisoned, and she was even sent into exile, but she nevertheless managed to carry on her espionage. All the while her fame increased, until she became a symbol of the Confederacy rather like Wisconsin's war eagle, Old Abe, was a symbol of the Union. She wrote her memoirs, *Belle Boyd in Camp and Prison*, when she was only twenty-one.

When the war was ending, Boyd took to the stage. Over the next three decades she married, outlived or escaped from various husbands, and traveled the nation as a celebrity. While performing in Kilbourne (now Wisconsin Dells) in 1900, she died and was buried there.

*Belle Boyd, confederate spy, shot a Union soldier when she was seventeen.*

*Milwaukee Sentinel,* January 7, 1923

# Summer Persecutions

When summer blazes in full force, those winter days when it seems like one's breath could freeze in the air, fall to the ground, and shatter are just a vague memory. But even summer has its unpleasantness, notwithstanding this description from a popular nineteenth-century handbook for immigrants: "Summer seems to burst at once upon us, and when it comes, the full and gorgeous foliage of the woods, and the exuberant luxuriance of the fields, give an idea of abundance and fertility which is delightful . . . the sun-sets in the State of Wisconsin, surpass even those of Italy and Greece."

Right.

But no romantic idealization can trump the eyewitness accounts of Wisconsin in the dog days of summer. The burning sun, algae blooms on the lakes, oppressive heat, dehydration, and exhaustion have been part of our heritage for centuries.

In the first week of July 1721, Father Pierre Charlevoix was traveling the shore of Green Bay when he found that "the sun was so hot and the water of the bay so warm that the pitch of our canoe melted in several places." And after the sun went down, there was relief from the heat but not from other forms of summer persecution: "To crown our misfortunes, the place where we halted for our encampment proved to be so infested with mosquitoes and gnats that it was impossible for us to close our eyes, although we had not slept for two days; and as the weather was fine and the moon gave us light we resumed our journey as early as three o'clock in the morning."

Charlevoix's contemporary, Sieur de Lamothe Cadillac, explained in 1718 in his *Description of Michilimackinac; Indian tribes of that region* how summer heat produced two names for the Ho-Chunk. The French used the word *Puans* for an Algonquian word they transliterated as "Ouinipegou," which has survived in the name Winnebago and which meant "ill-smelling": "The Puans derive this name from their river, which is very muddy. It is so full of fish of all kinds that it is difficult to understand how it can hold so many. Consequently during the heat of summer on account of either the quality of the water or the too great quantity of fish, the water is entirely covered with them and as it immediately becomes foul and putrid, it is hardly possible to approach the bank on account of the stench and the water is consequently very disgusting. It is for this reason that the nation is called that of the puans, for both in their persons and their habits they are the cleanest among the savages; and their women are the least dirty and are exceedingly careful to keep their cabins very clean and tidy, not a very common quality among other savage women."

Not much had improved a century later. On June 28, 1820, young James Duane Doty and four companions were being guided along the shore of Lake Superior by a pair of Indians in search of a huge copper boulder whose value had been the subject of many tales and speculations. At one point, they had to leave their canoe and hike overland. "I never underwent as great fatigue," Doty wrote in his diary. "The mercury in the thermometer stood at 90 in the canoe—on the mountains the heat was oppressive. To see the wind waving the tops of the trees without a single breath reaching us rendered the heat more intolerable. We passed several fine springs of water but our blood was so heated that we dared not taste them. At length we became so completely overpowered with fatigue & heat, the doctor particularly, that we were obliged to rest every 90 or 100 rods and when we arrived at the path I could not have gone 40 rods farther. . . . They led us directly to the rock or mass of copper which lies at the foot of the bank & close to the water. We were greatly disappointed as to size, its length being but 3 feet 8 inches, its breadth 3 feet 4 in, & its thickness about 10 or 12 inches, & containing 11 cubic feet as measured & computed by Capt. Douglass. The copper is embedded in stone of which I should think it did not compose one half; the copper might perhaps weigh one ton."

Intense summer heat also preceded the famous Peshtigo Fire, according to one witness: "In the year 1871 but little snow and rain had fallen and there had been an unusual drought. Forest fires had raged in many localities in August and September. The heat was oppressive and the smoke so dense that vision in broad daylight was seriously obscured on the waters of Green Bay. In full day-time mariners were compelled to resort to the compass to find their way into port. Flakes of black and white ashes and cinders fell in the streets of the city of Green Bay."

So as we struggle to cool off each summer, wiping away sweat and swatting at mosquitoes, you can rest assured that your forebears in Wisconsin went through much the same experience—just without air conditioning or refrigerators.

## The Voyageur with the Hole in His Side

On June 6, 1822, a shotgun blew a hole the size of a fist in young fur trader Alexis St. Martin's side. Military physician William Beaumont, who spent much of his career at Fort Crawford in Prairie du Chien, was astonished that St. Martin didn't simply die on the spot.

Instead, he recovered—though with a permanent opening through his muscle wall and into his stomach that required bandaging for the rest of his life. Unable to support himself as a voyageur, St. Martin went to work for Beaumont as a live-in handyman to chop wood and do odd jobs, one of which was to open up the window in his abdomen for scientific experiments whenever the good doctor commanded.

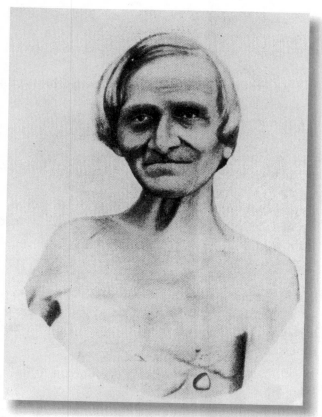

*Alexis St. Martin lived to age eighty-six with a hole in his abdomen open all the way to his stomach.*

Through that window Dr. Beaumont siphoned out gastric juices and inserted vegetables. He dangled bits of beef on a string, pulling them out after one, two, and three hours to observe the rate of digestion. Once, he put in twelve raw oysters.

For ten years Dr. Beaumont observed human digestion through the aperture in St. Martin's side. In 1833 he published a small book called *Experiments and Observations on the Gastric Juice and the Physiology of Digestion* that became a cornerstone of internal medicine. It also made the two of them famous, because until then no one had been able to figure out what happened to food after we swallow it.

Beaumont eventually left the military and moved to St. Louis, where he had a successful private practice. St. Martin lived fifty-eight years with the hole in his side, marrying and fathering several children and in his eighties becoming "very much addicted to drink," according to his lawyer. He died at age eighty-six on June 24, 1880, in St. Thomas de Joliette, Canada. Thinking he had suffered enough indignities in the name of science, his family let his body rot in the sun and then buried it in an unmarked grave so no further experiments could be performed on it.

# *Valentine's Callers*

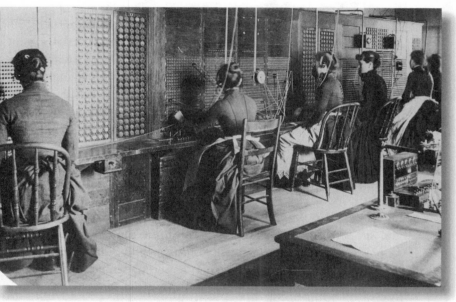

*Operators on the first telephone switchboard in Milwaukee, circa 1883.*

WHi Image ID 9215

$\mathcal{M}$any people realize that Wisconsin was a pioneer in the manufacture of electrical appliances. But few know that Wisconsin residents played key roles in introducing the telephone, too, thanks largely to Richard Valentine of Janesville.

In 1874 Valentine, a telegraph operator in Janesville, went to Chicago to see a man named Elisha Gray, who was experimenting with sending music over wires. On February 14, 1876—Valentine's Day—Gray and Alexander Graham Bell both filed patents for an "electric speaking telephone," but Bell was given rights to the device. Valentine, who'd strung a telegraph wire between his home and his brother's, stuck one of the primitive devices on either end of their telegraph line in 1877 and made the first Wisconsin phone call. Soon the two brothers had fifteen more people connected, and so was born the state's first telephone network.

Valentine's strange idea caught on. At the end of 1877, the Milwaukee City Council leased three of the devices from Alexander Graham Bell's company in order to connect the mayor's office with the police and fire departments. Not everyone in Milwaukee was sold on the idea, however. When Valentine presented the possibilities of telephone communication to manufacturers as a way to connect their factories and warehouses, he was laughed out of town. But so many people did want telephones that switchboards were needed to connect everyone together, and Valentine set up the first one in Wisconsin near Dartford, in Green Lake County, in 1878.

In 1879 Valentine held a demonstration of this remarkable new technology for lawmakers in Madison. Lines were strung over buildings and through trees to connect the capitol with Science Hall on the University of Wisconsin campus, and legislators at one end got to speak with professors at the other. The whole state was properly impressed, and Valentine's eccentric vision swelled into a wave of enthusiasm for the new device.

One of the people who caught that wave was Angus Hibbard, who perhaps did more than any other person to spread wires, switchboards, and connections across Wisconsin. He founded the Wisconsin Telephone Company, which extended wires among cities in the 1880s. Many years later he wrote a long memoir about those early days, when conversations went dead because Indians along the line helped themselves to bits of copper wire to make jewelry and first-time users were amazed.

In Wausau, for example, Hibbard demonstrated the telephone to two lumberjacks who were just in from the woods. After connecting with a caller on the other end of the line, he offered the phone to the pair. One of them held it up to his ear, "and said in a gruff unnatural voice, 'Hello!' and then dropped the instrument as if it had been red hot, exclaiming, 'Well, I'll be damned. Come on out of this, Pete! It said, "Hello yourself!" Can you beat that!' " A Swedish immigrant, amazed at the power of Hibbard's technology, blurted out, "By yiminy, she talks Swedish!"

In Milwaukee Hibbard at first employed telegraph messenger boys to connect callers at the switchboard, but he soon found their street-smart ways were not well adapted to polite customer service. Hibbard wrote in his memoir that, greeted by an unhappy phone customer, "the boys sassed back and telephone exchanges became, in many places, exchanges of loud and lurid language. . . . Boys would be boys and they seemed to have in them some kind of uncontrollable deviltry that made them practically unendurable as telephone operators. They became impossible, they blew up—and a cry for help arose in the land. At once from here, there, and everywhere came the girls. Almost at once, before we could realize it, the telephone girls were seated at switchboards in all parts of the country, giving such service as had not been thought possible before, smoothing out the difficulties and bringing down blessings on their heads."

Pauline Juneau, a switchboard operator who started about 1883, recalled in 1933 in the *Milwaukee Telephone News*, "Of course the work was very strange to us, but we weren't long in getting on to things. . . . We were kept busy all day long, as the number of subscribers was constantly on the increase and those subscribers certainly believed in using their telephones! . . . There was one customer who told me over the wire to 'keep my shirt on.' Naturally, I had intended to do that anyway, but I was highly insulted and reported the incident. . . ."

From that point onward the number of telephones and callers has grown steadily, until today they are ubiquitous. If he could see sweethearts connecting on their cell phones, Richard Valentine would probably be delighted at the way things turned out.

# A Workingperson's Answer to the Monday Morning Blues

Trouble getting out of bed in the morning? Famous naturalist John Muir has the solution you've been looking for—a bed that gets rid of you!

In a letter written years later, Grace Lindsley recalled a visit to Muir's dorm room in North Hall at the University of Wisconsin in the early 1860s, where she encountered his combination bed/alarm clock that tipped him onto the floor at the appointed time each morning. At the same time, another mechanism would strike a match and light a candle at the foot of the bed. Muir's room was full of innovative gadgets to help him maximize his college experience, and many of them could still prove quite useful today. One invention, a book stand that revolved after a preset time spent studying, led Lindsley's mother to remark that "he ought to have so arranged it that if he hadn't properly learned the lesson, a hand would come up and bop his ears."

*John Muir's revolving book stand and study timer, now on display in
the Wisconsin Historical Society's headquarters building in Madison.*

WHi Image ID 10983

70

# III
## Animal Antics

# A Harvest of Rattlesnakes, Ginseng, and Solitude

In 1906 middle-aged Sarah Hardwick inherited five acres of remote woods alongside the Mississippi River. No road led to the top of the bluff, yet there, all alone and miles from the nearest neighbor, the "none too brawny" Hardwick lived in a small cabin at the top of a hill.

She went into seclusion there, gathering herbs and growing vegetables amid the trees and getting cash for other necessities by clubbing rattlesnakes to collect their bounties. Hardwick had settled near the spot where Josiah Cleveland had made his name capturing rattlesnakes on the tip of his forked stick and selling his catch as a "sure cure for rheumatism" many years before. After his death, snakes still infested the woods in numbers that drove even hunters away.

Waves of the venomous snakes passed by Hardwick's cabin at times, and she kept a club beside the door to keep them at bay. For twenty-five years, she said, she was "always watching, always listening."

When a reporter visited her in 1931, most of the rattlesnakes were gone and she was supporting herself by raising ginseng. Having gathered seeds from a few wild plants some years before, she was able to cultivate a substantial crop to sell at fifteen dollars a pound, enough to purchase the few store-bought things that she wanted each year.

Of course, her needs were simple. She rarely came out of the woods, and she was proud of her solitary life. "I like to live away from town and be independent," she explained. When she did leave her cabin in the woods, it was usually to go down to the river and pick up a newspaper from a passing boat. "I like to read about England," she said. "My people came from there. My grandfather was an English bishop." Although the newspapers might be several months old, she said, "I read everything in them. I want to keep up with what is going on in the world." She just didn't want too much personal connection with it, as she rarely bothered to leave the woods.

When the reporter remarked, "But you are lonesome, aren't you?" she replied simply, "I never think about it."

# "Productive of a Good Deal of Profanity"

*Lake Mills pioneer Elisha W. Keyes*
*was well acquainted with "prairie itch."*

WHi Image ID 33715

74

$\mathcal{L}$ater generations heard a lot about the sufferings of the pioneers—spending cold winters in drafty log cabins, raising all their own food, hiking miles for simple necessities, and so on. But homesteaders faced more mundane trials, too.

"I know there was one trouble," wrote Lake Mills pioneer Elisha W. Keyes in a letter, "from which nearly all of the old settlers suffered which was attributed to a variety of causes. It was a disease that was never known to prove fatal, though it was very annoying and frequently productive of a good deal of profanity; but it had to be endured as patiently as possible for, as I remember, there were no means ever discovered to cure it. It really had to wear itself out. I allude to that affliction, which the old settlers certainly cannot have forgotten, known as prairie itch. It was very amusing at times to see a whole family out around a log house leaning against the butt ends of the logs, scratching first one shoulder and then the other, reaching points that they could not easily touch with their hands."

It was caused by microscopic parasites found in shallow water, such as that in low-lying fields. It produced bumps the size of mustard seeds, mostly on the neck and shoulders, and intolerable itching. One home remedy was a lotion made from the root of the aptly named skunk cabbage—an instance, perhaps, where the treatment was worse than the disease.

# Horrible Monsters That Devoured Men and Canoes

In May 1673 two canoes made their way down the west shore of Green Bay near Marinette, Wisconsin. They held French teacher and missionary Father Jacques Marquette, Louis Joliet (a young philosopher-turned-trader-turned-explorer with "the courage to dread nothing where everything is to be feared"), and three Native Americans who knew the terrain and were responsible for the explorers' safety. The group stopped in late May to consult with the Menominee Indians about their plan to search for a great river to the south or west. Their hosts "did their best to dissuade" them by saying that "the great river . . . was full of horrible monsters, which devoured men and canoes together; that there was even a demon, who was heard from a great distance, who barred the way, and swallowed up all who ventured to approach him." Fortunately, Marquette and Joliet were not deterred by these stories and pressed on anyway, traveling thousands of miles into the North American interior and confirming that the Mississippi River did indeed end in the Gulf of Mexico. They did encounter at least one monster on their trip, however, according to the diary kept by Father Marquette: "we saw . . . a monster with the head of a tiger, a sharp nose like that of a wildcat, with whiskers and straight, erect ears." So what horrible monster did Marquette see? Most likely, it was a species of large catfish.

*Marquette (standing) and Joliet exploring the Mississippi River, in a painting by Frank Zeitler.*

WHi Image ID 2344

# Runner Beats Horse in Milwaukee

When in 1875 a proud Irish gentleman proclaimed his new race-horse could beat all comers—knowing full well that his neighbors owned only draft horses—a crafty German tavern keeper proposed a race between the horse and a man. As recounted in the April 8, 1933, *Milwaukee Sentinel*, the man chose the course—a mile up the neighborhood's best-known thoroughfare, bounded by wooden sidewalks, and the runner—a wiry little tailor named Otto without an extra pound anywhere on his body. At the sound of the starter's shotgun, the barefoot tailor took to the boardwalk, the racehorse to the miry spring road, and . . . the tailor won, having run "fleet as a deer, stopping only to look around once or twice to see how near his opponent was." At the finish line he sat and waited for the racehorse, pulling a wooden sliver from his foot. The Irishman, a good sport, carried the tailor back to the tavern, where they all enjoyed a cold beer on him.

*A lively looking horse pulls a man in a cart through Milwaukee in this 1856 sketch by Franz Holzlhuber.*

WHi Image ID 28046

79

*Tarzan of Rhinelander?*

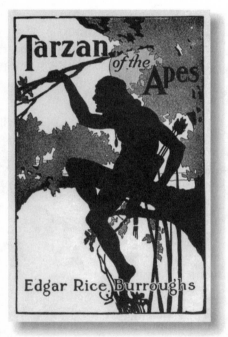

*In Burroughs's novel, Tarzan of the Apes swung through the trees of Nicolet National Forest to save Jane from a forest fire.*

Frontispiece to *Tarzan of the Apes* (New York: Grosset & Dunlap, 1914)

*". . . she had been carried off her feet by the strength of the
young giant when his great arms were about her in the distant
African forest, and again today, in the Wisconsin woods. . . ."*

So wrote Edgar Rice Burroughs in one of the most famous pulp
novels in American history, *Tarzan of the Apes*, first published in New
York by A. C. McClurg in 1914. Near the end of the book, the first
in a series, we learn that Jane Porter had spent her earliest years on
a farm in northern Wisconsin before venturing with her scientist
father across the Atlantic. After Tarzan rescues Jane in the African jungle and learns both English and French (and so much more
about "civilized life"), she abandons him by agreeing to marry an evil
creditor of her father. She goes to live with the villain in a farmhouse
left to her by her mother—in northern Wisconsin.

Of course, the story cannot end there, and a forest fire that
echoes Peshtigo's is introduced to liven up the narrative. Just as
her childhood home and Jane herself are about to be consumed by
the flames, Tarzan miraculously appears, swinging limb to limb
through what today is the Nicolet National Forest, to pluck her
from danger.

All this occurs in the book's penultimate episode, chapter
27, in which Tarzan also proposes marriage. Does Jane accept
"this jungle waif?" Could this good Wisconsin girl truly find
happiness with a "husband whose life had been spent in the tree
tops of an African wilderness, frolicking and fighting with fierce
anthropoids?" You'll have to read the book to find out.

# Terrapin Blues

**M**ilwaukee vaudeville entertainer and instrument maker Anton Hudy believed the crowning achievement of his career was fashioning a mandolin with a sounding board made from a snapping turtle's shell.

In the first decade of the twentieth century, Hudy and his wife entertained large audiences in Wisconsin's principal city, he on various stringed instruments and she playing the fine-tooth hair comb. "The spectators couldn't understand why I was combing my hair," said Mrs. Hudy. "Of course they didn't see the sheet of paper I concealed in one hand. Suddenly I would fold the paper over the comb and we would strike up a tune. You should have heard the crowds cheer!"

As the world of vaudeville changed after the arrival of moving pictures, Hudy spent years as an inventor and repairer of musical instruments before coming up with the idea of backing stringed instruments with turtle shells. At the time of a 1935 interview done by the *Milwaukee Journal*, Hudy was about to send his twenty-two-year-old son Frank around the Gulf of Mexico and down the coast of South America in quest of the perfect terrapin for musical purposes.

*Mr. and Mrs. Hudy hold the tools of their trade, a turtle-shell mandolin and a fine-toothed comb.*

Milwaukee Journal, November 24, 1935

# Toads and Flu Season

*F*eeling under the weather? You might want to try this mid-nineteenth-century treatment for "smallpox, the plague, or any eruptive fever" from Madison doctor Hugh P. Greeley (and retold in the September 11, 1921, *Milwaukee Journal*): "In the month of March, take toads as many as you will, alive; put them in an earthen pot, so it will be half full. Cover it with a broad tile or iron plate. . . . Put charcoals around about it . . . set it on fire and let it burn out and extinguish of itself. When it is cold, take out the toads, and in an iron mortar pound them very well and searce [sift] them. Pound and searce them again. The first time they will be brown powder, the next time black. Of this you may . . . drink inwardly in any infection taken." On second thought, you probably can't find the major ingredient at this time of year. The good doctor also recommended the application of a wildcat skin for pain.

# IV
# Political [Im]Ponderables

# DANGER!

## Woman's Suffrage Would Double the Irresponsible Vote

# Bench and Barroom

The first judge to preside over the federal district court in Milwaukee "was 6 feet in height, with a large head and red face, depicting his intemperate life. . . . He was very irascible, had a most violent temper, and was as unsociable as a bear."

The Honorable William C. Frazier arrived in Madison for a court term in July 1838 and "insisted on opening the court and holding the term as the law required," John Catlin, the court clerk, recalled in Daniel Durie's *A History of Madison, the capital of Wisconsin* (1874). "I informed him that there was no business, and no lawyers in attendance. He said that made no difference; it was necessary to adopt rules, and accordingly the court was opened."

Not only were criminals and attorneys lacking, but so, too, was Frazier's other necessity—a good stiff drink. The only liquor found in Madison was a supply of "Chinese cordial" stored for medicinal purposes. "The whole set was emptied by the judge while holding the term, about a dozen bottles, and when the cordial had all leaked out, the judge took his departure and never held another," wrote Catlin.

In Milwaukee, Frazier ruled so capriciously that local attorneys called for his resignation, "which called forth such a flow of blasphemy as probably never came from the mouth of a judge." After a session in Green Bay, he returned to Milwaukee on the steamboat *Pennsylvania*, and when she anchored in the bay, the judge, "who was dead drunk at the time, was lowered by means of a tackle into a boat and rowed to the landing." He never recovered from his bacchanalian revel and died on November 8, 1838, from his overindulgence.

## Bergerisms

The nation's first elected Socialist congressman was quite a quirky character. Not one to let high office or honors change him, Victor Berger remained a "man of the people," eating pie with his fingers, wearing flashy suspenders, and even getting his nails manicured when he first went to Washington—all traits that helped to take the symbol of Milwaukee socialism off his pedestal and onto the barstool.

And, in the same vein as the oft-seen touristy saying, "My grandma went to [insert: fun place] and all I got was this crappy T-shirt," Berger, upon retiring from the Socialist national executive committee, remarked, "I have been a member of the committee since the party was organized and all I ever got out of it was a twenty-year prison sentence." (Berger's antiwar stance earned him a conviction in 1919 for violating the Espionage Act; the conviction was overturned in 1921. Berger never served a day of the sentence.)

*Victor Berger, Milwaukee's Socialist congressman, received a prison sentence for his political beliefs but was reelected anyway.*

WHi Image ID 1901

# Briefest Chief Executive

*M*ost Wisconsin residents know that Tommy Thompson was the longest-serving governor in state history. But who has the distinction of occupying the executive office for the *shortest* time? That honor goes to Arthur McArthur, who was governor for a mere five days in 1856.

McArthur (1815–1896) was born in Scotland and came to Wisconsin in 1849 to practice law, quickly getting involved in Milwaukee politics. Democrats had controlled the state for years, and when incumbent Democrat William Barstow ran for reelection as governor in 1855, he chose McArthur to run as lieutenant governor. Their only serious opposition came from Coles Bashford of Oshkosh, the candidate of the brand-new Republican party, formed in July 1854. The Democratic machine thus assumed an easy victory, as usual.

But the Republicans took them by surprise. The incumbent Barstow won by such a slim margin that the Republicans not only claimed victory themselves but also charged the Democrats with vote tampering. On January 7, 1856, *both* Barstow and Bashford claimed to be the true governor of Wisconsin, and *both* of them held swearing-in ceremonies. The supreme court investigated and found that ballots had indeed been tampered with: returns supposedly sent from outlying counties had in fact been written on paper used only under the capitol dome, and vote totals had been tallied from northern townships where no voters actually lived.

As the evidence of fraud mounted against Barstow, he withdrew from the race on March 21, 1856, which left his lieutenant governor, McArthur, as the state's chief executive. On March 25 the supreme court gave its final ruling in the case and named Bashford Wisconsin's governor. Tensions had run so high that when Bashford arrived at the capitol that day to assume the office, he brought along a sizable contingent of muscular friends. After calmly hanging his coat in the official gubernatorial coat closet, he told McArthur that he'd come to take possession. "Will force be used?" McArthur asked. "I presume no force will be necessary," Bashford replied, "but in case any be needed, there will be no hesitation whatever, with the sheriff's help, in applying it." McArthur beat a hasty retreat to the sound of jeers and hoots from an assembled crowd.

So ended McArthur's brief tenure as a Wisconsin governor—though not that of his political career. During the Civil War, McArthur was known as a "War Democrat" and subsequently joined the Republican Party. In 1858 he was elected a Wisconsin circuit court judge and served in that capacity until he was appointed by President Grant to a similar position in Washington, D.C., in 1870. Altogether McArthur spent more than a quarter century on the bench. He retired in 1887 but remained prominent in national Republican circles, "fond of dining out, and always ready with a fund of stories to amuse" as noted by the *Milwaukee Journal* in December 1942. McArthur was the father of the famous Civil War general Arthur MacArthur (1845–1912, who changed the spelling of the name) and grandfather of World War II hero General Douglas MacArthur (1880–1964). He devoted his final years to reading and writing about English history and literature until his death in Atlantic City, New Jersey, on August 26, 1896.

*William Barstow and Coles Bashford both claimed*
*the governorship in 1856.*

WHi Image ID 38567 and WHi Image ID 38566

# Chicago, Wisconsin?
## It Could Have Happened

When the founding fathers imagined the Midwest (then known as the "Northwest") in 1787, they agreed that any north-south border between new states should be "drawn through the southerly bend of Lake Michigan." If their plan had been carried out, everything north of the line from Gary, Indiana, to Davenport, Iowa, would be in Wisconsin today, including the Illinois cities of Rockford, Galena, and even Chicago. But when Illinois became a state in 1818, national politics twisted fate in another direction.

At the time, slaveholding Southern states and free Northern ones were wrestling for control of Congress. Whenever a new slave state was admitted to the Union, opponents would balance it with the admittance of a free state. So when Mississippi entered in 1817, Northerners hustled to compensate for the imbalance. Illinois seemed like their best bet. But most of Illinois's population lived in the Ohio Valley, an area more closely aligned with the South, which caused one leading politician to warn, "In case of national disruption, the interest of the state would be to join a southern and western confederacy."

If Illinois had a Great Lakes port, however, its northern half could develop business ties to New York and New England and lessen the overall Southern influence among its people. Northerners therefore moved the border sixty miles north in 1818 to give the new state a city on Lake Michigan. Although what is now Wisconsin was robbed of 8,500 square miles, there were too few U.S. citizens living in the area at the time to protest. That "national disruption" ultimately came in 1861, forty-four years after it was first discussed, after Illinois delivered the presidency to Lincoln and went on to fight the Union rather than joining the Confederate cause. Losing Chicago was probably a small price to pay for that greater gain.

## Constitutional Labor Pains

Seeing the rose-colored treatment our nation's founding and its founding fathers receive, it may be tempting to see Wisconsin's official founding that way too: noble, dignified, and bathed in amber-colored light. No, Wisconsin's birth was more like a ragtag assemblage of pioneers of varying (or no) qualifications attempting to invent first a territorial government and then, a decade later, a full-fledged state government.

For example, in late October 1836 the first territorial representatives met in Belmont, in southwestern Wisconsin. "I find as I anticipated," Henry Baird (1800–1875) wrote in a letter home, "a great want of legal talent. . . . The representation is however, for a new country, by no means despicable, and much superior to my expectations." In another letter written a few days later, he fears that "feelings of distrust and jealousy . . . may materially interfere with our deliberations" and undermine the whole attempt at forming a viable state. But after a few weeks of shady wheeling and dealing, the capital was located at Madison, and the government met there the following summer. This newborn baby called "Wisconsin" learned to crawl and then to walk during the 1830s and 1840s, as squealing pigs beneath the legislative chambers and a gunfight by disputing lawmakers occasionally brought proceedings to an unexpected halt.

When the time came a decade later to draft a state constitution, delegates wrangled for weeks to come up with a founding document that would meet everyone's wishes, pitting such diverse figures as a Southern lead miner, a French fur trader, and a Yankee real estate speculator against each other. The 1846 constitution that emerged from the wrangling was a utopian document full of socially advanced notions such as that married women should be allowed to own property and that black residents should be allowed to vote if a popular referendum endorsed the idea. When citizens turned out to vote for or against the new constitution, the majority rejected such radical propositions and delegates went back to the drawing board. Two years later voters accepted a sanitized constitution that made no mention of women's rights, and Wisconsin became the thirtieth state.

*Our first territorial capitol, at Belmont, 1870.*

WHi Image ID 10476

# Cure for Long-Winded Politicians

When Wisconsin's second Madison capitol building was finished in 1869, an enormous chandelier was suspended from the ceiling of the west wing. Lawmakers felt nervous sitting beneath it, though, so it was soon removed, leaving a hole in the ceiling. After twenty years, a small mountain of dust and grime had accumulated around the edges of the hole, directly above the heads of the elected officials.

One day in the early 1890s, as a particularly verbose legislator droned on for hours, a bored colleague imagined how he could put all that dust to good use. He secretly instructed a page to lay a heavy plank across the hole, propped up on a stick, and to run a cord from the stick down to a nearby closet. The next day, when yet another speaker launched into an oration threatening to last for hours, the inventor snuck off to the closet and gave the cord a sharp tug. The plank crashed down with a deafening thud and "a stifling cloud of dust shot out from the hole and scattered over the members below," according to the *Sheboygan Press Gazette*, December 13, 1924. "There was no more talking that day."

After that, the overhead silencer became something of an institution in the Wisconsin assembly. A page was assigned to reset it regularly, and some lawmakers even brought umbrellas to their desks to protect themselves from the shower of dust. As a result, legislators learned to express themselves in the fewest possible words, and if any member left the room during a speech, the legislator, with anxious glances at the ceiling, usually picked up the pace and brought his speech to a hasty conclusion.

*The assembly room of Madison's second capitol building. The chandelier marks the spot of the "overhead silencer" in the top center of the image.*

WHi Image ID 23440

## *Dangerous Radicals*

$\mathscr{D}$ateline: Watertown, Wisconsin, 1912. Extremism is nothing new in Wisconsin politics. This poster attempts to halt a dangerous "Menace to the Home, Men's Employment and to all Business." The question is, if woman suffrage doubled the irresponsible vote, who made up the other half of it? (By the way, the antisuffragists won the 1912 round.)

*An argument against woman suffrage, 1912.*

WHi Image ID 1932

# Father-Son Senators

*A*ccording to the U.S. Senate's history site, the first and only father and son to serve in the Senate at the same time were Henry Dodge of Wisconsin and his son Augustus Caesar Dodge of Iowa. The elder Dodge represented Wisconsin in the Senate from 1848 to 1857. When he arrived in Washington, he joined his son, who was already there as an Iowa senator (1846–1855). So for seven years in the middle of the nineteenth century, the Senate had its only father-son team.

Henry Dodge grew up near St. Louis and moved to Wisconsin in 1827, settling with his slaves near the present site of Dodgeville in order to mine lead. He led the local militia in the Black Hawk War, was appointed governor of the territory of Wisconsin, 1836 to 1841, and was elected as a Democrat to the House of Representatives for the Twenty-seventh and Twenty-eighth Congresses (March 4, 1841–March 3, 1845).

The elder Dodge returned to Wisconsin to serve a second time as governor of the territory (1845–1848), and then, when Wisconsin became a state in 1848, he was elected to the United States Senate. He served in the Senate from June 8, 1848, to March 3, 1857, where he chaired the Committee on Commerce before retiring. He died in Burlington, Iowa, June 19, 1867.

Augustus, Henry's son, was born in 1812 and followed his father to the Lead Region in the 1820s. In 1837 he moved across the Mississippi to Burlington, Iowa, which he represented in the U.S. House of Representatives until the end of 1846, when the territory of Iowa was admitted as a state. The younger Dodge was then elected as a Democrat to the United States Senate, where he served until 1855, when he was appointed U.S. ambassador to Spain (1855–1859). He died in Burlington, Iowa, in 1883.

*The only father–and–son senatorial team,*
*Henry and Augustus Dodge.*

WHi Image ID 2613 and WHi Image ID 45758

# Injudicious Appointment

In 1803 a man who "manifested his lack of business ability" through successive failures became sole government representative of the land that would become Wisconsin—and all without a copy of the territorial statutes. Charles Reaume (1752–1822) was a failed merchant, farmer, and fur trader who fled to Green Bay from Montreal or Detroit about 1792. On the recommendation of an acquaintance (based on who knows what qualifications), territorial governor William Henry Harrison appointed Reaume justice of the peace, and until 1822 Reaume dispensed idiosyncratic justice according to French and Indian customs rather than U.S. law.

Once, when two Frenchmen appeared before him over disputed property, he refused to rule in favor of either but found them both culpable and delivered this sentence: "You, Boisvert," to the plaintiff, "bring me one load of hay; and you, Crely [the defendant], bring me one load of wood. And now the matter is settled."

Another time the judge met a defendant stopping to buy him a bribe, a small coffee pot, on the way to court. "Go away, go away," Reaume protested, "I have given judgment against you." But the defendant persisted and gave the judge the gift anyway, saying, "But judge, I don't owe that fellow anything." Reaume, coffee pot presumably in hand, replied, "You don't? The rascal! I reverse my judgment, and he shall pay the costs."

Reaume, who lived in the Green Bay region, was much loved by many French Canadians and Indians, but he was considered pompous, arbitrary, and lazy by the few English-speaking Yankees who had begun to settle in there. One of them recalled that "a bottle of spirits was the best witness that could be introduced into his court" and that after the decision of a case, if the losing party produced such a witness, a new trial or a reversal of the former decision was often obtained. Many defendants found themselves sentenced to labor a certain number of days on his farm, or to cut and split a certain number of rails for him. Juliette Kinzie (1806–1870), whose recollections entitled *Wau-Bun* are a classic of early Wisconsin, called him "excessively ignorant and grasping, although otherwise tolerably good-natured."

In 1810 Reaume moved up the Fox River to a trading post near modern Kaukauna, where, according to biographer James Lockwood's *Early Times and Events in Wisconsin*, he "sold liquor to the Indians, not unfrequently drinking freely with them, and sharing in their frays, as well as in blackened eyes and bruises. There he died alone, in the spring of 1822 . . . about seventy years of age." He was buried in an unmarked grave at Green Bay.

*Juliette Kinzie, who called the early territorial justice of the peace Charles Reaume "excessively ignorant and grasping."*

WHi Image ID 2398

# "I Struck Out Right and Left," Confesses Lawmaker

"Congress has become little better than a den of semi-savages," reported the *New York Tribune* in 1860, a determination that may have been partly the fault of a Wisconsin congressman. On February 8, 1858, a bloody melee broke out in the House that brought fame to Representative John F. Potter of Milwaukee. The House was engaged that day in a heated debate—as many were in the days leading up the Civil War—over sectional issues. Northern representatives outnumbered those from the South, and they pressed their parliamentary advantage, infuriating the few Southerners present. A fistfight between two members quickly turned into a general brawl, and the House floor, according to Potter, became "strewn with men." During the fray, Potter managed to pull the wig off an opponent's head. At this, a cry went up in the gallery that Potter had "taken a scalp," and the Southerners made a rush at him. "I struck out right and left and then fell down," Potter confessed. After things settled down, Potter was covered in blood and marked by Southerners as an enemy. His exploits on the floor that day had even garnered the attention of a pacifist Quaker congressman, who asked Potter if he had taken lessons in the "pugilistic art." When Potter said no, the man responded, "I notice thy blows were very effectual."

Potter found himself embroiled in another incident in April of 1860, when, following another fight, he was challenged to a duel by a notoriously bellicose Virginia representative. Potter accepted the challenge and insisted that the duelists wield bowie knives, "at a distance of four feet." His challenger, Representative Roger Pryor, beat a hasty retreat, and Potter received gifts of bowie knives from sympathizers all over the country, earning the nickname "Bowie-knife" Potter.

*This enormous bowie knife was a gift to Milwaukee Representative John "Bowie-knife" Potter, after he challenged a Virginia representative to a duel.*

WHi Image ID 45547; Wisconsin Historical Museum #1957.1122

# La Follette at the Fire

*E*very Wisconsinite knows of the political accomplishments that earned Robert La Follette the moniker "Fighting Bob," but few know that Fighting Bob also fought fires. Awakened in the middle of the night on February 27, 1904, La Follette, governor at the time, was informed by fireman John Brahany that the capitol was on fire and that they needed help from Milwaukee. La Follette dressed and rushed downtown into the burning building, where for three hours he helped evacuate government records and other valuables. Nearly everything of value was saved, including the portraits of former governors that hung in the capitol building hall. At 11:00 a.m., he was buttonholed by a *Wisconsin State Journal* reporter, who described La Follette as "excited" and "nervous" as he gazed at the ruins behind him.

*The capitol fire of 1904.*

WHi Image ID 1906

107

# Lawless Legislators

*L*aws are the basis of society, right? The words in our statutes define what we must, can, and must not do. Our police make people comply with laws, and our judges punish those who don't, by referring to what the law says. That's why it's odd that for the first few years of Wisconsin's existence, not even the legislators who made the laws could get their hands on a copy.

They certainly tried. When Wisconsin became a territory on July 4, 1836, the laws of Michigan Territory as printed in the *Revised Statues of Michigan* remained in effect. Few copies of this book had ever left Detroit, however.

The Wisconsin laws passed during the first session of the territorial legislature in Belmont in 1836 were printed in a little pamphlet of eighty-eight pages, but that didn't include the Michigan laws that still governed the bulk of public affairs.

So when the lawmakers met for the second time, in the winter of 1837–1838 at Burlington, Iowa (Madison's capitol not being finished yet), they ordered that all of the Michigan laws pertaining to Wisconsin Territory should be printed alongside the ones they themselves had passed.

Unfortunately, communications technology was so primitive that no local printer could manufacture such a book. The one they hired, James Clarke, found himself unable to fulfill his contract,

*Henry Dodge, the first territorial governor, ran Wisconsin without written laws for several years.*

WHi Image ID 2613

and in the spring of 1838 he went east to Pennsylvania to get the book printed. When lawmakers convened again in June of 1838, they heard testimony "that Mr. Clarke left Burlington destined for some of the eastern cities, taking along with him several extracts from the statutes of Michigan, as he supposes, for the purpose of procuring the printing of them in pamphlet form; and to await the arrival, after they should have been prepared for that purpose, of the manuscript copies of the laws passed" in the current summer session.

But the legislators decided that Clarke had failed to honor his contract and hired another Iowa printer. He agreed to print the extracts from the Michigan statutes, the laws passed in the winter 1837–1838 session, and those passed at the current summer 1838 session, "the whole to be done up in one volume to be half bound in calf, and fifteen hundred copies thereof to be delivered . . . within seventy-five days."

When lawmakers sent for their fifteen copies seventy-five days later, their agent reported back, "I am sorry that I am compelled to inform you that the laws . . . are not even yet entirely printed. . . . It would not probably be practicable to send them to your territory until the opening of navigation in the spring." Once again, the legislators were disappointed—and still without printed laws.

Meanwhile, Clarke, the first printer, had managed to get copies manufactured back East but "owing to the low stage of water in the Ohio they have not been received and will not probably arrive before spring."

The frustrated legislators—who had started passing laws in 1836 and more than two years later still hadn't received a reliable printed version of them—sent a messenger from Madison to Green Bay to search for copies of the Michigan statutes and "to procure for the use of the legislature such numbers as may be had of copies of these laws." At least that way they'd have some part of the laws to refer to during their deliberations.

And while they waited, they formed a committee to put together from scratch a new and revised edition of the complete laws of Wisconsin Territory, to be published in 1839. In the spring, some copies of Clarke's first compilation and some copies of his successor's arrived, but by then their half-finished, ad hoc publications had been made obsolete by the comprehensive 1839 edition.

By the time that edition was ready, the Wisconsin Territory had functioned for two and half years without lawyers, judges, citizens, or even the legislators themselves being able to cite the text of any law by which their society was governed.

# Original State Constitution Missing!

*D*ateline: Madison, Wisconsin, 1848. Ever wanted to see Wisconsin's original constitution? Sorry, you can't, for the hand-written manuscript of our state constitution is lost! That crucial document, the foundation of our legal system and government, resides in historical oblivion. This catastrophe was apparently first reported by the *Milwaukee Sentinel* and picked up some time later by Madison's *Capital Times*. The first to discover it missing was historian Lyman C. Draper, who tried to track it down in 1882. He contacted Morgan L. Martin of Green Bay, one of its signers, and Martin replied, on May 19, 1882, "My own impression favors the idea that the first secretary, McHugh, gave the original to the printer for copy, and that it was not returned to the office." The official printer at the time was Horace A. Tenney of Madison, but the manuscript of the constitution was apparently not among his papers when he died. By the 1930s officials speculated that the constitution might have found its way into the congressional library or the Smithsonian, though a thorough search of both had not produced a single clue to its whereabouts. At present, the state operates under what "purports to be, and no doubt is, a copy of the constitution," written on vellum in a copperplate hand at the same time as the original.

# Horrors! Page the Liberty League!
# Wisconsin's Constitution Is Gone!
# State Officials Start Search

**BY GABRIEL J. TOLAN**
[Of The Capital Times Staff]

WHERE is Wisconsin's original constitution? That is a subject which is a subject which is today puzzling state officials.

Investigation in the secretary of state's office yesterday revealed that the famous document, outlining the rights of the people and establishing governmental procedure, is missing.

Every effort to trace the lost document has failed. Recently, officials thought it might have found its way into the congressional library or the Smithsonian institution, but a thorough search of these two places failed to disclose a single clew to the whereabouts of the famous paper.

The constitution was adopted in a convention held Feb. 1, 1848. It was ratified by the people on Mar. 13, 1848; the state was admitted to the union May 29, 1848, and the first state officers took office June 7, 1848.

At present the state is operating under provisions of what purports to be, and no doubt is, a copy of the constitution.

Whether some early-day souvenir hunter walked off with the original constitution, or whether it was left with the printer is not known today. Many believe that it lies, dust covered, on a shelf in some old Wisconsin home, where some day it may come to light.

A copy of the constitution, which is kept tucked away in a tin container in the vaults of the capitol, looks like a big calendar. Hand written, the document does not contain the signatures of the original signers.

The only list of signatures of the original signers of the constitution is found in an auditor's book compiled about the time the constitution was drafted. Among the signers were James Fagan, William H. Fox, C. M. Nichols and M. L. Martin, who was chairman of the constitutional convention.

One page of the constitution states: "writs of error shall be prohibited." Today writs of error are common in court procedure.

One of the earliest books on record in the vaults of the secretary of state is a volume containing the territorial laws of Wisconsin passed in the November session of the legislature in 1836. In those days the legislature, made up of the legislative council and house of representatives, met every year instead of every two years.

Among the laws passed was a measure to amend an act governing appointment of sheriffs and a bill calling for the establishment of ferry service on the Mississippi river at Eagle Point.

At that time, P. J. C. Engle was speaker of the house. It was decided at this session to have the legislature meet on the first Monday of November each year.

People were talking about railroads in those days. The legislature gave permission to David Morgan, L. Martin and James Doty to incorporate the La Fontaine Railroad Co., with capital stock of $50,000.

Wisconsin's record of Civil war deserters is an amusing one despite the serious aspect of the charge of desertion. Wars must have been as unpopular then as they are now, because the huge book containing the names of deserters lists hundreds who ran away from the battle fronts of Bullrun and Gettysburg.

*Capital Times,* October 31, 1938

# The Other First President

February 22 is not only George Washington's birthday but also a big day in the life of our nation's only *other* first president. On February 22, 1862, Jefferson Davis was elected president of the Confederate States of America, thirty years after launching his career in Wisconsin.

Fresh from West Point, Davis arrived at Fort Crawford in 1828. His first assignment was to cut timber on the Red Cedar River in northwestern Wisconsin for repair of the fort at Prairie du Chien. Later that year, he moved to Fort Winnebago at Portage, where according to a *Milwaukee Sentinel* article he was recalled as a "lean, lank, imperious, overbearing first lieutenant." While there, he met and fell in love with a young Indian woman. He soon became jealous of another of her admirers, a Green Bay boat builder named Stewart, and when the two came to blows, Davis was beaten into humiliating submission in front of the entire garrison.

His true love, however, was Sarah Knox Taylor, the daughter of his commanding officer at Prairie du Chien, future U.S. president Zachary Taylor. Against her parents' wishes, she married him, and he resigned his commission. They set up housekeeping on a cotton plantation in Kentucky.

One of Davis's last acts in Wisconsin was to escort the defeated Sauk chief Black Hawk to prison in 1832. Black Hawk recalled that his party "started for Jefferson Barracks, in a steamboat, under the charge of a young war chief, who treated us all with much kindness. He is a good and brave young chief, with whose conduct I was much pleased."

*Jefferson Davis, first president of the Confederate States of America, began his army career in Prairie du Chien and Portage.*

WHi Image ID 33475

# Poverty at the Supreme Court

In the nineteenth century, Wisconsin Supreme Court justices were paid so little that some of them had to go into debt merely to keep house in Madison. The city's chief banker, Lucien Hanks, who started as a humble teller in 1860, recalled that many officials died almost in penury.

We tend to think of such august figures as pillars of their community—wealthy, learned, and as a stable as Wisconsin bedrock—but Hanks shows some of them with their suspenders down, on the edge of bankruptcy.

In December 1923 the *Wisconsin State Journal* reported that Luther S. Dixon, who became chief justice in 1859, told Hanks he "came to Madison from Portage, easily worth $15,000" but a few years later was forced to borrow money just to meet the cost of serving on the supreme court. Justice Byron Paine, who had defended Sherman Booth, arguing successfully that the Fugitive Slave Law was unconstitutional, and in the 1865 Ezekiel Gillespie case won the right of black citizens to vote, came trembling into the bank unable to make ends meet and not knowing where to turn. Hanks suggested a life insurance policy through the company he represented, but Paine, at first, declined. The next morning, Paine returned to Hanks's office with news that "Mrs. Justice Payne has handed down her decision, that if your offer is still open, it be accepted."

Yet another time, Hanks was called to the office of Chief Justice Edward G. Ryan, where he found the judge "walking up and down the room, alone, and evidently very much disturbed, sans coat, sans vest, suspenders hanging over his thighs." Hanks managed to set Ryan's disastrous financial situation right.

## The Radical Women of Richland Center

Meeting with a secret agenda in the home of Laura B. James (mother of future suffrage leader Ada James) on a June afternoon in 1882, a group of Richland Center women formed Wisconsin's first woman suffrage club. As the wives of prominent businessmen and professionals, these women felt that their husbands might not approve of their activities, so they operated publicly as a social, philanthropic, and intellectual club—neglecting to mention the *exact* intellectual topic that brought them together. Publicly, the club advertised meeting topics on the "Life of William of Normandy," the "Education of Girls in China," and "Home Duties." In truth they discussed, among other things, marriage. As Mary Elizabeth

Hussong noted in the December 21, 1924, *Milwaukee Journal*, one club member came to the radical conclusion that "girls should be taught not to think that marriage finishes existence."

Woman suffrage had little popular support in nineteenth-century Wisconsin, but by the 1890s a new generation of suffrage activists led by, among others, Ada James of Richland Center began relying heavily on woman's clubs like this one to promote suffrage as one part of a broader platform of reforms.

*Ada James continued the fight for woman suffrage in Wisconsin begun by her mother in 1882.*

WHi Image ID 1991

# Two Years Before Seneca Falls

*I*n the autumn of 1846, when enough pioneers had settled in Wisconsin to form a state, they sent delegates to Madison to write a constitution. The delegates prepared a draft containing the radical provision that "All property, real and personal, of the wife, owned by her at the time of her marriage, and also that acquired by her after marriage, by gift, devise, descent, or otherwise than from her husband, shall be her separate property."

A woman allowed to own property? Keep her own wages? Have her own bank account? Had Wisconsin gone mad?

That's what Racine attorney Marshall Strong thought. "When the husband returns at night," he said in a debate at the constitutional convention in 1847, "perplexed with care, dejected with anxiety, depressed in hope, will he find, think you, the same nice and delicate appreciation of his feelings he has heretofore found? Will her welfare, and feelings, and thoughts, and interests be all wrapped up in his happiness, as they now are? . . . Will the word 'home' sound as sweetly? Where will be its guardian angel? O, sir, the effect of this law upon the husband, upon the wife, upon the children, and upon all the domestic relations will be most fearful."

Wisconsin voters—all male, by definition—agreed with his logic, and in April 1847 they rejected the draft of the constitution.

Not until 1921 would the legislature grant women full equality with men under the law, and Wisconsin's was the first such equal rights law in the nation.

# V
# Palatable Peculiarities

# And You Thought Your Vegetable Garden Was Out of Control

August in Wisconsin for home gardeners and cooks often means bumper crops of zucchini, cucumbers, tomatoes, and more. As you think of clever ways to bless your neighbors with piles of squash, just imagine trying to deal with the vegetables that came from the imaginary garden of Alfred Stanley Johnson Jr., a Waupun photographer who specialized in the production of tall-tale postcards. In these images, produced between 1911 and 1917, Johnson staged friends and family in elaborate backgrounds that he later embellished with enlarged vegetables and fruits.

Wisconsin's bountiful soils were a primary selling point for town promoters seeking to lure new settlers and immigrants in the nineteenth and early twentieth centuries. Immigrant guides lavishly praised the state's agricultural potential, often citing examples of amazing crop yields and profit earned in Chicago, Cleveland, and other eastern markets. Johnson's tall-tale postcards attributed the astounding agricultural achievements pictured to the fertility of Wisconsin soils and the skills of local farmers.

*There are plenty of potatoes for everyone . . .*

WHi Image ID 44616

*Crazy cows leap off the roads near Madison.*

WHi Image ID 44422

*Waupun's giant onions.*

WHi Image ID 44418

*A large cargo of cabbage.*

WHi Image ID 44445

# Death by Chocolate — Really

As Ella Maly left a party in Richland Center on January 8, 1891, she was given a bag of chocolates as her parting gift. She ate several pieces on her way home before collapsing in agony. After hours of convulsions and delirium she uttered, "If this would be the end of me, I would be so thankful!" and died—from strychnine poisoning.

Her party host had been twenty-four-year-old Rose Zoldoske, a Sunday school teacher who boarded with a widowed doctor. Zoldoske was accused of murder. At her trial, it was revealed that she was in love with the doctor and had considered Maly a rival. Worse, further investigation revealed that the doctor's wife had also died from strychnine poisoning soon after Zoldoske came to live with them. Her case drew national attention. "But for her sex," the press reported, "she would have undoubtedly been lynched."

Despite Zoldoske's seeming link to the two deaths, nothing connected her to any strychnine, and nobody saw her poison any chocolates. She cut a fine appearance in court and favorably impressed the reporters. The jury, however, found her guilty, unleashing fistfights between partisans and widespread pleas for clemency.

After Zoldoske spent six years in prison, Governor William Upham pardoned her on his last day in office. Early in 1897 she fled to a remote farm miles from any train station to spend the rest of her life in obscurity. The press asked, "A modern Lucretia Borgia or a victim of circumstantial evidence?" After more than a century, the jury's still out.

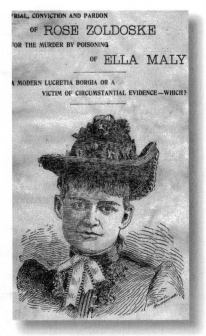

*The presumed poisoner of Richland Center, Rose Zoldoske.*

*Milwaukee Sentinel*, February 28, 1897

*A Dinner Plate Full of Patriotism*

The Women Students' War Work Council and the UW Home Economics Department produced this recipe booklet to help families ration wheat, sugar, dairy products, and meat during WWI.

*War Time Recipes.* (Madison, Wis.: Women Students' War Work Council of the University of Wisconsin, 1917.) WHS Pamphlet Collection, PAM 54–1139

*C*ould you live without wheat, beef, pork, dairy products, and sugar? While this may sound like fightin' words in a dairy and agricultural state, during World War I Wisconsin citizens were encouraged to do just that—and the Women Students' War Work Council and the UW Home Economics Department produced a booklet of recipes to show you how.

Although most people associate food rationing with World War II, state and federal ration programs were first implemented as a show of home-front patriotism during the First World War. In fact, Wisconsin pioneered many of the programs that formed the foundation for federal Food Administration policies. Wisconsin became the first state to organize both state- and county-level councils of defense, which helped to educate citizens about wartime sacrifices. Wisconsin's State Council of Defense was particularly interested in the national food crisis that developed once the United States entered the war in 1917. Council chairman Magnus Swenson began vigorously promoting food conservation through the cultivation of home gardens and the institution of meatless and wheatless days.

Anyone for some steamed barley pudding?

# A "Gibraltar of the Wets"

Though known as the Dairy State, Wisconsin might just as easily have been known as the Brewski State, because beermaking was a tradition in many communities around the state. In 1921 the state passed the Severson Act to enforce the federal prohibition provision (ratified in 1919); it was quickly denounced by progressive governor John J. Blaine. In a 1926 popular referendum, Wisconsin voters overwhelmingly supported an exemption for 2.75 percent "near beer," and in 1929 voters endorsed another that called for an end to prosecutions under the Severson Act.

By then federal officials were afoot in Wisconsin to assess conditions. Investigator Frank Buckley found that Wisconsin was "commonly regarded as a Gibraltar of the wets—sort of a Utopia where everyone drinks their fill and John Barleycorn still holds forth in splendor." After ten years of Prohibition, he found that in Madison, "The section of the city known as the Bush is made up of Sicilian Italians of the worst sort, most of whom are bootleggers. . . . The queen of bootleggers, an attractive young Italian girl caters exclusively to a fraternity-house clientele. While in Madison the writer visited the local chapter of his national fraternity (D.K.E.) one morning about 9 o'clock. Quite a commotion was observed at the time, as a result of an attempt to induce two

*Celebrating the end of Prohibition, 1933.*

WHi Image ID 9426

of the brethren, who had apparently imbibed well but not wisely the night before, to get up for morning classes."

Other cities were worse. At the opposite end of the state, Hurley, "tucked away up in the wild lumber and iron section of northern Wisconsin, right on the Michigan State line, has the distinction of being the worst community in the State. Conditions in Hurley are not unlike those of settlements like Dawson City, Cripple Creek, El Dorado, Borger, and other boom communities. Gambling, prostitution, bootlegging, and dope are about the chief occupations of the place. Saloons there function with barmaids who serve the dual capacity of soda dispenser and prostitute." Of course, by the time poor Frank Buckley visited Hurley in 1929, the world had known ten thousand years of gambling, drinking, and prostitution, and no mere amendment to the U.S. Constitution was likely to change human nature.

By then, too, former governor Blaine had become a U.S. senator and was making a national reputation for himself with calls to repeal the Eighteenth Amendment. After a dozen years of seeing breweries go bankrupt and organized crime taking their place, of watching innocent drinkers be poisoned by black market moonshine, and of having misguided government interference turn otherwise law-abiding citizens into criminals, voters came around to his point of view. On February 28, 1933, Congress passed an amendment repealing Prohibition, and it became law on December 5, 1933, when Utah finally ratified it. Wisconsin was the second state to approve the amendment on April 25, marking the demise of our nation's most enthusiastic effort to regulate public morality.

*Java Man*

***Charles Clark, coffee king.***
*Milwaukee Journal,* September 27, 1942

*D*o you worry that you drink too much coffee? Charles Clark of Milwaukee literally spent his life at it. He got into coffee just as consumers switched from roasting their own beans to buying preroasted and ground beans at the grocery store. After starting in the business in New Orleans in 1885, Clark moved to Milwaukee in 1902 and opened the Clark & Host coffee roasting company. For decades he spent part of each day surrounded by cups, sniffing the aroma of the freshly roasted beans and then brewing and sampling to make sure that his product was up to snuff (so to speak). He soon became a national figure in the coffee industry, becoming president of the National Coffee Roasters' Association (an organization he had, incidentally, helped to organize) in 1922. After nearly six decades in the coffee business, he retired in 1942 and sold his company to Roundy's Supermarkets—contenting himself to whatever coffee his wife brewed at mealtime.

# More than One Way to Skin a Cat

*D*ateline: Prairie du Chien, Wisconsin, 1848. Prairie du Chien claims to have had Wisconsin's first temperance society, and with this honor came some of the first attempts to circumvent its members' watchful eyes. Keeping liquor away from the determined soldiers at Fort Crawford proved nearly impossible, even with the vigilance of the officers and temperance society. One moonlit night, John Fonda and Major John Garland were out for a stroll after inspecting the troops for the evening when an object in the distance attracted the major's attention. "Is that a cat going toward the Fort?" he asked. Supposing it was only a cat creeping across the green, Fonda paid no more attention to it. But as they got closer, Garland's attention was again drawn to the cat, and they wandered over to see why it was moving so strangely.

Upon closer inspection, they discovered a string stretching from the fort's wall toward the cat. When the major stepped on the string, the cat stopped. Garland picked up the cat and found that it was not a cat at all but a cat's skin stuffed with a bladder full of whiskey. And here the major had just been remarking on the unusually sober appearance of the soldiers living at the fort.

# Mr. Wright's Second Slice of Pie

Frank Lloyd Wright had a justifiably large ego and a personality of mythological proportions. He is even said to have been the inspiration for Ayn Rand's famous self-appointed prophet Howard Roarke in *The Fountainhead*. In 1942 William T. Evjue, founder and editor of Madison's *Capital Times*, visited Wright at his home in Spring Green and discovered another side of the man. Wright led Evjue on a private tour of his home, Taliesin, followed by dinner "cooked by the young men and women of the fellowship" using food grown on the property.

It was during dessert that Evjue learned that, beyond any architectural accomplishments, Wright was "a true son of America" when he heard Wright ask for a second piece of pie: "Do you know of anything that more quickly places the label of American on a man than when he asks for the second slab of pie—and pumpkin pie at that!" wrote Evjue in the *Capital Times* on October 20, 1942. Wright's simple wishes were categorically overruled by his wife, Olgivanna, however, with the admonition that "Every time Frank eats the second piece of pie he always says later, 'I wish I hadn't eaten the second piece of pie tonight.' " But in Evjue's book, "the fact that Frank Lloyd Wright wanted that second piece of pie placed him along with Daniel Webster who once said: 'I was born an American; I will live an American; I shall die an American.' "

# New Year's Celebration in Madison, 1851

It was a nineteenth-century custom to open one's home on New Year's Day and entertain with refreshments and best wishes anyone who came to the door. On January 1, 1851, two young Madison men vowed to visit—and eat or drink something at—every house in the city. Lawyer Elisha Keyes and his companion, Willet S. Main, started out bright and early on their task, making calls that were "necessarily of brief duration" while never skimping on time spent at the refreshment table. Typically, coffee came first, then bread and butter followed by some cold turkey, doughnuts, and cake. Every once in a while, "a good old fashioned mother would regale the boys with a piece of genuine old time mince-pie, which was always received with great satisfaction," Keyes recalled in the *Madison Democrat* on December 31, 1899. In the end, they visited one hundred tables, a "big day's work" for two enterprising young men.

*Early Madison lawyer Elisha Keyes.*

WHi Image ID 37908

137

# Sex, Drugs, and Rock and Roll, circa 1700

We sometimes like to think that our own age is unique in its level of moral corruption, but whenever lust and greed have been given free rein, human nature sinks toward its lowest common denominator. In 1702 Father Etienne de Carheil reported to his superiors in a letter that lust and greed had corrupted nearly everyone connected with the fur trade on the Wisconsin frontier. Fur trade voyageurs, hunters, explorers, and merchants have been romanticized so often that we benefit from seeing the trade's dark side through his eyes.

Voyageurs traveled "from one mission to another, making the savages drunk and seducing the women in all the Cabins where they lodge." The commerce in brandy and women had brought the "missions to the brink of destruction"—so much so that Carheil despaired that "we no longer have occasion to remain in any of our missions up here, to waste the remainder of our lives and all our efforts in purely useless labor, under the dominion of Continual drunkenness and of universal immorality." He called on the French government, then the "owner" of Wisconsin, to end the excesses of profiteering, drunkenness, gambling, and debauchery that threatened the future of France's project in North America.

*Artist's depiction of voyageurs encamped.*

WHi Image ID 3776

# Take Some Diastoid and Call Me in the Morning

*O*riginally developed as a nutritional supplement for infants and people with bad digestion, malted milk changed the way America ate. Pharmacist James Horlick developed his wheat- and malt-based drink in London but soon moved to Racine to join his brother William. In 1873 the two formed a company to manufacture their own brand of infant food. Ten years later, the Horlicks patented a new formula enhanced with dried milk that they marketed under the name "Diastoid." Although the name didn't last—the company trademarked the name "malted milk" in 1887—the drink surely did, becoming a soda fountain staple.

Despite its origin as a health food for infants and invalids, Horlick's malted milk found several unexpected markets. Explorers like Admiral Richard E. Byrd appreciated its lightweight and high-caloric qualities that allowed it to travel worldwide. Byrd was so fond of malted milk that he even named a mountain range in Antarctica after the Racine company.

*Horlick's Malted Milk was made in Wisconsin but traveled the globe;*
*Admiral Richard Byrd took Horlick's to Antarctica.*

WHi Image ID 23703

*Water: Quenching Your Thirst and Healing Your Pain...*

*The Fountain Spring House hotel associated Waukesha's spring with the famous waters of Saratoga to draw tourists.*

Wisconsin Historical Society Pamphlet Collection, PAM 57–1825

*M*ineral springs, known for their unique medicinal and therapeutic properties, played an important role in the early tourism and resort industry in Wisconsin, particularly in Waukesha. Known as the "Saratoga of the West," Waukesha's history was forever changed in August of 1868 when Colonel Richard Dunbar drank twelve tumblers of water from the spring at Bethesda and proclaimed his incurable diabetes gone. Dunbar's "miracle" brought trainloads of visitors to Waukesha and led to the development of hotels and resorts to house all those who came seeking miracles of their own. Soon, other "healthful" resorts began springing up all over Wisconsin and the upper Midwest, prompting the Chicago, Alton & St. Louis Railroad to issue travel guides to the healing waters along their rail lines in 1875. Waukesha water was even pumped all the way to Chicago for the Columbian Exposition in 1893, showcasing to the world the wonder that flowed beneath the town.

In the nineteenth century, many Americans traveled to distant springs to drink, bathe in, and totally immerse themselves in the supposedly healing powers of hot and cold mineral waters. Doctors analyzed newly discovered springs and constructed elaborate scientific classification systems and health regimens based on water cures. The discovery of germs and bacteria in the early twentieth century, though, changed the way that medicine understood and treated disease, leading to a decline in the use of miracle waters.

*The Dunbar family at the Bethesda spring, 1875. Richard Dunbar, "cured" by the miracle spring, is seated near the center.*

WHi Image ID 45659

# When Beer Was (Almost) Illegal

*P. T. Barnum: showman, circus celebrity . . . and Prohibition promoter?*

Wisconsin Historical Society's Circus World Museum

While most people know that alcohol was outlawed for a time in the 1920s, prohibition had actually been on the table much earlier in Wisconsin. Strange as it sounds, in November of 1853 a majority of Wisconsin voters chose to outlaw liquor consumption. Statewide, the vote was 27,519 to 24,109; in Milwaukee, where beer was a vital part of German culture, the vote went the other way: almost ten times as many voted against prohibition as voted for it.

That fall, circus promoter and celebrity P.T. Barnum had toured Wisconsin in support of prohibition. His fame, imposing appearance, charisma, and sheer enthusiasm won many citizens over to the cause of temperance. He couldn't win the legislature, however, where enabling legislation was required to turn the public referendum into law. State senators and assemblymen were afraid of alienating German voters and feared being seen as allies of utopian reformers (dangerous radicals who wanted to abolish slavery and let women own property). They refused to act on the referendum, and Wisconsin's prohibition legislation died in committee.

# When Romance and Style Came with a Full Tank of Gas

While driving excitement is today intimately tied to the car itself, in the 1920s fantastic-style filling and service stations provided attention-grabbing design and romance for motorists traveling Wisconsin roadways. Functioning as three-dimensional billboards, thematic gas stations were readily identifiable for their resemblance to pyramids, windmills, and tepees, among other designs.

In Wisconsin, Wadhams Oil Company used the intrigue of the East to create an ornate pagoda-inspired chain of stations across the state. More than one hundred stations were constructed between 1917 and 1930, and though varying in floor plan, all featured a red-stamped metal roof with flared eaves. The Wadhams pagoda represented an early effort to tie architecture to corporate image, a move that would soon become a staple of fast-food architecture.

*The 1920s Wadhams pagoda-shaped gas stations brought the exotic East to Wisconsin roadsides.*

WHS Historic Preservation Image

# VI
## Spiritual Encounters

# The Crowning of King James

*J*uly of 1850 marked the high point of one of Wisconsin's oddest stories.

James J. Strang (1813–1856) was an early Mormon leader in the years before the Latter Day Saints emigrated to Utah. After the death of founder Joseph Smith in 1844, Strang forged a document claiming that he had been selected by Smith to be his successor. The community divided on this question, with some of the faithful following Strang while the majority followed Brigham Young. Young led his contingent to Utah, and Strang led his to . . . Wisconsin, where they founded the colony of Voree (1844–1847) near Burlington in southeastern Wisconsin and later established a "kingdom" on Beaver Island (1847–1856) in northern Lake Michigan, where more than one thousand of the faithful assembled. It was there in a tabernacle built of logs that, on July 8, 1850, Strang had himself crowned "king of earth and heaven."

Sectarian infighting and hostile attacks by neighboring "Gentiles"—some of whom were outraged at the islanders' polygamous arrangements—disrupted this 1850s idyll. Among other things, outrage over Strang's dress code eventually led to his downfall. Strang decreed that all women were to wear ankle-length calico pantalets with a knee-length skirt overtop. When two women refused, Strang ordered their husbands whipped. The act aroused such indignation that a plan was hatched to assassinate the king, which was accomplished on July 9, 1856. After Strang's assassination, the community soon dissolved, though sincere adherents to his teachings lived on around Voree until at least the 1970s.

*Early Mormon leader James Strang's Burlington house, site of his first Wisconsin colony.*

WHi Image ID 29670

# The Ghost and Mr. Nadeau

*I*n the summer of 1834, Reverend Cutting Marsh of Kaukauna journeyed across Wisconsin into Iowa, keeping a daily diary as he traveled. While on the Mississippi he heard about the recent death of "a very wicked man" named Nadeau, whose fate seemed worthy of a story by Edgar Allan Poe:

"It was said," Reverend Marsh wrote on August 23, "that he and his wife a few years ago killed a Menominee woman and cut her almost all to pieces with a knife, and then threw her into the river. Ever since then he had been afraid to be alone in a room, but would run out as tho frightened at something—was horribly profane and a drunkard. At times he would look round and start on a sudden, and run saying that the dead and the devil were after him."

The Indians among whom the unfortunate Nadeau moved certainly believed that the ghosts of those slain in battle or other occasions haunted their killers. To escape from them, Sauk and Fox warriors would run around their village three times and then wash themselves before entering, and the ghosts would leave them alone.

Monsieur Nadeau apparently didn't know about this technique, and his friends and family became concerned about his mental health. They found him a job on a Mississippi River steamboat, which they hoped would keep him occupied: "At times they were fearful that he would make away with himself, and so they watched him; but a day or two before his death, he was at work on a steam boat. They got him to do this thinking to divert his mind. But nothing availed to erase from his memory the heinousness of his past offence."

Marsh, a strict Congregationalist, believed that we are all sinners in the hand of an angry God, and he concluded that "judgement, it would seem, lingered not. A night or two after this he died in a sitting posture, as I was informed, holding himself up having his hands clasped round a post or stake stuck in the ground!! 'But o their end, their dreadful end!'" (a quote from the hymn "The Prosperity of Sinners Cursed" by eighteenth-century author Isaac Watts, based on Psalm 73).

Marsh concluded his diary entry with the terse note, "Was much disturbed during the night and slept but little."

# Ghost Country

Route 151 winds through Wisconsin's best-known ghost country. The stretch from Dodgeville to Blue Mounds became so famous for hauntings that by 1943 folklorists had collected several hundred tales of "the Ridgeway Ghost." Though most were undocumented, one incident appeared in the *New York Times* (December 7, 1902).

The paper reported that John Lewis, "a prosperous farmer living in the vicinity of Ridgeway, a man of sober life, [and] undaunted courage," cut through the fields one night after helping a neighbor with some butchering. Climbing a stone wall, "his attention was arrested by the sight of a figure that seemed to have gathered itself together out of the just now tenantless air and stood confronting him in a menacing attitude."

Lewis fled, but the ghost stepped across his path and raised its arm. "Next morning a neighbor found Lewis lying inside the wall in a semi-conscious condition. . . . He said he had been hurled in the air as if in the vortex of a cyclone, pounded, crushed into insensibility. He died a few hours after he was carried home, asserting with his dying breath that he had come to his end by a supernatural agency."

Many local residents gave accounts like this between 1840 and 1900. Although reports of the Ridgeway ghost declined over the decades, claims of mysterious manifestations occurring as late as 1993 have surfaced on the Internet. The supposedly haunted house collapsed in ruins a few years ago, but legends about its ghostly occupant live on.

## Gideons Began in Badger State

Open any hotel nightstand drawer, and you are bound to find a Bible placed there by Gideons International. The Gideons have been around for more than one hundred years and actually began in a hotel room in Wisconsin.

On a September evening in 1898, two traveling salesmen met by chance in a Boscobel hotel. With the hotel crowded to its limits, the manager asked John Nicholson of Janesville and Samuel E. Hill of Beloit to share a room. In room 19 of the Central Hotel, the men discovered that they were both Christians. They prayed and read the Bible together before settling down for the night. They reflected on the fate of salesmen spending long days on the road and lonely nights in strange beds, and they talked about starting an organization for Christian traveling men like themselves but parted ways before they made any plans.

A chance meeting of the two men at a Beaver Dam hotel on May 31, 1899, rekindled the idea of an association. As reported

*The Boscobel hotel where traveling salesmen John Nicholson and Samuel Hill originated the idea of the Gideon Society.*

WHi Image ID 29567

years later in the *Madison Daily Journal* of August 12, 1923, faced with barrooms and worse temptations in towns across the country, Nicholson and Hill vowed to "surround the arch enemy of our souls and give him a black eye." So with Babbitt-like zeal (and a regrettable fondness for clichés), they decided to "get right at it. Start the ball rolling and follow it up." They held their first meeting on July 1 in Janesville and founded the Gideons, named for the man who was willing to do anything God wanted.

As traveling men, the question of how best to serve God in the hotels where they spent most of their time naturally arose. They soon came up with the idea of putting a Bible in every hotel room, with specific passages recommended to their era's equivalent of jet-lagged businessmen.

Three decades later, a survey of hotels discovered that many of these volumes were being used simply to prop up windows on hot summer nights or to steady a wobbly bed frame. But many others showed well-thumbed pages and worn bindings, and in one Milwaukee hotel a battered copy bore the poignant inscription, "God bless my mother, who is so far away. R.S."

The Gideons are still alive and well, handing out more than sixty million Bibles each year in 181 countries.

# Holding Church Down at the Depot

*A*ccording to the May 27, 1923, *Milwaukee Journal*, pioneer telegrapher and railroad worker George F. Brigham (1827–1914) of Sharon, in Walworth County, performed many feats in his long life. This onetime telegraph operator in Sinclairville, New York, and for the Erie railroad knew the inventor of the telegraph, Samuel F. B. Morse, met President Fillmore and Senator Daniel Webster, and strung wires with the man who would later found Cornell University. He received the first telegraphed message of a presidential inauguration, that of Zachary Taylor (once a Wisconsin resident himself) in 1849, and thus was in at the birth of the modern news industry. He helped establish the first electronic communications system for a railroad and sent the first telegraph signal to dispatch a train.

When Brigham moved to Sharon just after the Civil War to serve as station agent, he found that the town had no Episcopal church. So, he combined his job as station agent with the ministry and held lay services in the waiting room of the train depot until he could raise enough money to erect a church. Ordained an Episcopal priest at the age of seventy-five in 1902, he continued to hold Sunday services at his church in Sharon until he was well into his eighties.

# Juliet Severance, Radical Victorian

While many people like to think that hippies invented free love, communes, and health food in the 1960s, like most others those ideas have a history, and some of their proponents are part of Wisconsin's history.

Whitewater physician Juliet Severance was born in 1833 in western New York, the nation's hotbed of reform and Utopian thinking. At an early age Severance got interested in the antislavery movement, temperance, and women's rights. She became a schoolteacher and used her rhetorical skills not only in the classroom but also as a speaker at rallies and conventions at a time when few women appeared in such public roles. Concluding that slavery, gender equality, and substance abuse were primarily moral issues rather than political ones, she joined the Baptist church as a young woman.

When her health suddenly began to decline, Severance decided to study medicine and apprenticed herself to a local physician. She then attended college for three years in New York and graduated in 1858 with her MD at age twenty-five. She believed that scientific medicine failed to explain or treat disease effectively, and she explored then-new alternatives such as vegetarianism and psychic healing. Throughout her career, she gave free medical care to working women. Encounters with a medium in college shook her faith in the traditional Christian explanation of the spirit world, and reading Thomas Paine and Charles Darwin (as soon as *The Origin of Species* appeared) put an end to her career as a Baptist just before the Civil War.

In 1862 she moved to Whitewater, where she quickly set up a flourishing medical practice. Whitewater at the time was a center of mystic experiments and the "spiritualist" movement, and her views on life, health, and politics found a receptive audience there. To her list of radical causes she added abolition of the death penalty (already the law in Wisconsin but not elsewhere) and of the institution of marriage. Like her better-known contemporary Victoria Woodhull, Severance argued that traditional marriage oppressed women and threatened their moral, legal, medical, and spiritual well-being. This didn't stop her from marrying and raising a family of her own, but then, her husband was a freethinking vegetarian ("He never eats meat, fine flour bread, or butter [but mainly] grains, fruits and vegetables, and cereals") and a radical like herself.

After the Civil War, Severance moved to Milwaukee, where she took up labor reforms in addition to her religious, health, and women's rights work. She became an official in the Knights of Labor and a delegate to three national conventions of the Labor Party, during one of which (1888) she introduced a plank for woman suffrage into the party platform. All this political agitation and committee work gave her skills in parliamentary procedure that were much in demand, and she served as director, president, and board member of many organizations. She was the president at various times of the State Associations of Spiritualists in Illinois, Wisconsin, and Minnesota, and in 1880 she was elected first vice president of the Liberal League, a national organization of freethinkers led by Colonel Robert G. Ingersoll.

In 1891 Severance left Wisconsin for Chicago, where she continued to practice medicine. She ultimately moved to New York to live with her daughter and kept up her reform activities until her death in 1919. A few days before she died she was volunteering at the Red Cross and writing an article for a radical magazine called *The Truth Seeker*.

At the height of her career, her colleague Victoria Woodhull described Severance as "a radical of the radicals. In religion she is a Free Thinker of the Spiritualistic school. Politically, she believes in individualism against nationalism, and she is especially interested in the emancipation of women from every form of serfdom, in church, State or home."

# Mary Hayes-Chynoweth, Psychic Healer

"I was crossing the kitchen with a basin of water when, suddenly, some unknown Force pressed me down upon my knees, helpless," Mary Hayes-Chynoweth told her biographer about the spring day in 1853 that changed her life. "Of my own will I could not move nor see nor speak; but a compelling Power moved my tongue to prayer in language or languages unknown to me or to my father," who was reading the Bible in the same room. A twenty-seven-year-old schoolteacher in Waterloo at the time, Hayes-Chynoweth was told by the Power that she would spend the remainder of her life healing others, and for the next half century she devoted herself to the practice of spiritual medicine.

Hayes-Chynoweth (1825–1905)—she married Waterloo farmer Anson Hayes in 1854 and, after his death, Madison attorney Thomas Chynoweth—was one of Wisconsin's best-known psychics during the decades when spiritualism swept across the nation. Séances, spirits knocking on tables, communications with the dead, and other supernatural phenomena caught the public interest in the mid-nineteenth century. Hayes-Chynoweth regarded most of these events as hoaxes or distractions, relying instead on the unique powers that she felt were channeled through her by God.

She explained that divine power allowed her to see right through the human body and other material objects as though they were transparent, enabling her to pinpoint the cause of a disease. To heal the sick, she would take the patient's symptoms into her own body, routinely breaking out in their blisters, rashes, or tumors while they themselves recovered. She prescribed a variety of herbs and water treatments for the sick and taught that the keys to health were optimism, faith, a diet mostly of vegetables and grains, and total abstinence from alcohol, tobacco, coffee, and tea.

Throughout the Civil War era, she crisscrossed southern Wisconsin conducting healing sessions. Among those who believed in her skills and came to her for advice or healing were U.S. Senator William Vilas, Wisconsin Supreme Court Justice William Lyon, and Wisconsin Historical Society superintendent Lyman Draper. Except when putting her sons through college as a single mother in the 1870s, she never charged any fees for her services but rendered them free to everyone who came to her, patiently enduring in her own body her clients' painful symptoms. Hayes-Chynoweth took no personal credit for her skills but merely saw herself as the medium through which a universal power of love and life could be expressed for the benefit of others.

The "Power," as she called it, manifested itself in ways other than healing the sick. Under its influence, she was seen to speak to patients in languages she didn't know, including German, Polish,

*Mary Hayes–Chynoweth, psychic and healer.*

WHi Image ID 45757

and Danish. She could foresee some future events, including visitors en route to her, economic depressions, and market prices, allowing her family to capitalize on its wheat crop in a time of crisis.

In the spring of 1883, Hayes-Chynoweth told her sons, who were starting their legal practice in Ashland, to sell off a forest tract they'd bought as a logging investment and use the profits to buy acreage along the Montreal River. The Power had told her their fortunes lay in mining, and it pointed her to a specific location forty miles from Ashland in the middle of the wilderness. When her sons protested that they knew nothing about mining, she reassured them that they would soon meet someone to help. One of their clients turned out to be the only geologist who had explored the Gogebic Iron Range, and he agreed immediately to show it to them.

When Hayes-Chynoweth heard their accounts and saw their maps, the Power told her exactly where to dig, and they sunk shafts each time directly into some of the richest iron ore in the Gogebic Range. The family's Germania and Ashland mines not only made them extraordinarily rich but also helped create the town of Hurley, for which Hayes-Chynoweth felt personally responsible. When she saw Hurley's tavern owners growing rich by ruining the health of the town's workers, she established a school where the laborers could learn to read and write. Many became mine foremen or engineers, and six went to college, all at her personal expense.

In 1887 she, her sons, their families, and many of her followers moved to a large estate in San Jose, California, where they formed a colony called "Edenvale." There she spent most of the next two decades producing a journal called *True Life*, overseeing the family's business affairs, and receiving admirers and patients. In the early 1890s she treated an average of 3,500 people per year, most of whom doctors had abandoned as incurable. When the 1888 mansion burned to the ground, she replaced it with a 41,000-square-foot, 240-room edifice that is today used as a conference center.

In 1905, at the age of eighty, Mary Hayes-Chynoweth finally passed away, her physical body worn out but her emotion and spirit intact.

Most of the evidence for the life of Mary Hayes-Chynoweth comes from *The Spirit Dominant: A Life of Mary Hayes Chynoweth* by Louisa Johnson Clay, written by a grateful client based on interviews with Hayes-Chynoweth and her patients and published by her sons about 1914.

*Whitewater's Morris Pratt Institute, also known as "Pratt's Folly,"
the only spiritualist school in the world.*

Milwaukee Sentinel, March 6, 1921; image courtesy of Fred G. Kraege

167

When religion and science clashed in the 1850s, reactions were varied. Some people gave up ancient dogmas with a sigh of relief, while others dug in their heels and insisted on the literal truth of "old-time religion." A few simply lost their faith and spent the rest of their lives searching for it again.

Among these were people who thought that science might help discover the truth about the soul, life after death, and other spiritual questions. Wisconsin was not immune to this spiritualist fervor, and one of the movement's best-known advocates was Morris Pratt (1820–1902) of Rock County.

Born in 1820 in New York, he moved to Milton as a young man and built a successful farm. In the 1850s, when séances, spirit knockings, mediums, and trances came into fashion, Pratt embraced these new "revelations" enthusiastically and vowed that if he was ever wealthy he would give his fortune to support the scientific teaching of spiritual truths. Long after the general public had concluded that spiritualism was unsound or uninteresting, small colonies of devotees remained in Whitewater, Lake Mills, Waterloo, and other southern Wisconsin towns—and Morris Pratt could always be found at their meetings.

Around 1884, Pratt—one of those fortunate friends of psychic Mary Hayes-Chynoweth, who sometimes advised friends regarding financial opportunities—invested his modest savings in property in northern Wisconsin. The land turned out to contain some of the richest iron ore in the Gogebic Range, and within a few months Pratt was able to sell his shares for more than two hundred thousand dollars. He had become wealthy almost overnight.

True to his word, Pratt began building an eighty-thousand-dollar edifice in downtown Whitewater to house his spiritualist institution in 1888. Known locally as "Pratt's Folly," the building was finished but not occupied until after his death in 1902, when the Morris Pratt Institute registered its first students. Its curriculum consisted of the typical slate of conventional courses but was augmented with classes in psychic studies, mediumship, and the science of séances. The school still exists today, relocated in West Allis, and one can enroll there to study clairvoyance, telepathy, mediumship, and psychic surgery, among other subjects. Its graduates can go on to serve as clergy in one of the dozens of churches that belong to the National Spiritualist Association.

# Mysterious Woman of the Woods

The toughest work in lumber camps was done by oxen, who hauled huge sleds of massive tree trunks out of the brush and over the snow to the nearest river. When spring came, the winter's harvest along with many of the lumberjacks floated downstream to the company mill. One lumberjack, however, had the lonely task of driving the herd of oxen through the forest and back to the milltown.

A young man named Delos Washburn was given that job in the early spring in the 1860s. His crew had spent the winter in the wilderness seventy miles northwest of Green Bay, where Forest, Langlade, and Oconto Counties meet. When his mates started downriver with the logs, he started overland with the oxen along a crude path through the forest, the only road in any direction for many miles. He brought along a load of hay for the beasts and enough food to hold him for several days, when he expected to reach Oconto.

At the end of the first day, nightfall overtook him in the vicinity of the modern village of Mountain, which is about midway between Wausau and Peshtigo. The oxen, not used to having their freedom, had been hard to keep on track, and even after he had fed them, eaten his own dinner, and settled down next to the fire, one of them wandered off into the woods. Washburn was reluctantly pursuing the animal, calling it by name and coaxing it back to camp, when to his amazement a voice answered his own: "Don't be afraid; he won't go far." And into the campfire's circle of light stepped a solitary young woman.

Washburn was astonished. The only road in all of Oconto County was this narrow logging track through the woods. The nearest houses were twenty-five or thirty miles away, where a couple of hardy families had settled at Gillett. To make things even stranger, the woman didn't know her own name, where she came from, or how long she had spent in the wilderness all by herself.

A few days later, the pair reached their destination in Oconto. None of the residents recognized the woman, and as officials questioned her it became clear that she was mentally deranged. Either she had wandered off from caretakers somewhere and had become lost in the woods, or her experiences in the wilderness had permanently unhinged her memory and reason.

They concluded that she was harmlessly insane, named her Crazy Jane, and provided her room and board in exchange for work as a servant in the county jail. For years they asked passing travelers about her, hoping to discover some family who were searching for a long-lost girl or woman. But no one could ever shed any light on her origins or explain how she had walked out of the woods into Delos Washburn's camp, many miles from any road or settlement.

Jane enjoyed her work, performed it competently, and, although she slept in the jail, came and went freely around the village. She became a town character, and for decades everybody in the neighborhood knew Crazy Jane and her story.

Then one winter night, when she was past middle age and had become a well-established fixture in the community, she didn't return to her bed in the county jail. Jane vanished just as abruptly as she'd appeared. Residents searched the city and the surrounding area, but they could find no trace of her. Finally, in the spring, a hunter far out in the marshes along Green Bay came upon her corpse. It was concluded that she had wandered off, become lost in the darkness, and died of exposure in the night.

Her friends in Oconto could never find out any more about her, and Jane's true identity and origins remain a mystery to this day.

## Mystic Meeting of Madison Minds

Today, his scraggly hair, white beard, and granny glasses make James Davie Butler look like an aging Hell's Angel. In his day, however, Butler (1815–1905) was probably the most civilized man in Madison.

Butler was raised in New England, where he attended the seminary with plans to become a priest. But he instead moved west in 1858 to teach Greek at the fledgling University of Wisconsin. Relieved of his duties in 1867, he hopped the first transcontinental railroad simply for adventure. Getting off in California, the bookish professor hiked into Yosemite Valley, missed the trail, and promptly got lost in the wilderness.

Amazingly, his former student John Muir, enjoying his famous first summer in the Sierra, "was suddenly, and without warning, possessed with the notion that my friend, Professor J. D. Butler, of the State University of Wisconsin, was below me in the valley." Muir scrambled down from North Dome and came upon Butler "in the brush and rocks, half erect, groping his way, his sleeves rolled up, vest open, hat in his hand, evidently very hot and tired." Butler cried out, "John Muir, John Muir, where have you come from?" In his 1913 biography *The Story of My Boyhood and Youth*, Muir described guiding Butler to safety, calling it "the one well-defined marvel of my life of the kind called supernatural."

Muir returned to the woods and Butler to Madison, where he produced dozens of books, wrote thousands of articles (more than two hundred for *The Nation* alone), and never missed a Madison Literary Club gathering. On his eighty-eighth birthday, 166 admirers called to wish him well, and two years later he died at his home on Langdon Street, much loved.

*Lost in Yosemite Valley, former University of Wisconsin professor James Butler stumbled upon his former student, John Muir, in 1867.*

*James Davie Butler*, by James Reeve Stuart, 1888;
Wisconsin Historical Museum #1942.62

# Perpetual Praying Begins in La Crosse

The Franciscan Sisters of Perpetual Adoration in La Crosse have been praying nonstop for more than 120 years. Tag-team continuous prayer of praise, thanksgiving, and petition keeps at least two sisters at the altar twenty-four hours a day, seven days a week. The order was founded by members of the Third Order Secular Franciscans who left Ettenbeuren, Bavaria, in 1849 to do missionary work in America. Bishop Martin Henni of Milwaukee welcomed them into his diocese. When the Church formed a diocese for the counties around La Crosse in 1869, Bishop Michael Heiss requested that the sisters move their motherhouse. So in 1871, the sisters moved into their new motherhouse, St. Rose of Viterbo Convent, in La Crosse. The sisters assumed the title Franciscan Sisters of Perpetual Adoration on August 1, 1878, when, at 11:00 a.m., they began their perpetual adoration of the Eucharist. They have been praying nonstop longer than any other religious body in the United States and maintain a perpetual adoration clock on their Web site.

6631. St. Rose Chapel, LaCrosse, Wis.

**The St. Rose Chapel in La Crosse, where the Franciscan Sisters
perpetually pray.**

Wisconsin Historical Society Archives, Wisconsin Postcard Collection

# Vision of the Virgin Near Green Bay

SISTER ADELE

*Sister Adele became a nun after seeing the Virgin Mary
twice in Green Bay.*

*Milwaukee Journal,* August 3, 1919

There have been numerous sightings of the Virgin Mary and Jesus all over the world. Wisconsin, too, has been the site of mystic visions. In 1858, outside Green Bay, the Virgin Mary appeared to a young Belgian immigrant twice, exhorting her to give her life to serving others. The girl, Adele Brice, followed that advice and became a nun. Sister Adele spent the next four decades building a chapel, school, and orphanage on the site where the Virgin Mary spoke to her. And each year, thousands of people make the pilgrimage to the little town of Aux Premier Belges in Brown County on August 15, the anniversary of Sister Adele's sighting.

## A Wisconsin Ghost Town

Just below Blue Mounds State Park lies the forgotten settlement of Pokerville. The town sprung up shortly after Ebenezer Brigham settled near modern-day Cave of the Mounds in 1828, and during the Black Hawk War of 1832 settlers from miles around rushed into its hastily built blockhouse for safety. In the Wisconsin "Lead Rush" of the 1830s, Pokerville was on the main route between the mines and Milwaukee, and ox-driven wagons creaking under tons of lead stopped regularly. The town soon boasted two inns, several stores and bars, a blacksmith, a harness maker, and a doctor.

As in most frontier boomtowns, "Gambling was rife," wrote a Lucile G. Bohren in the *Wisconsin State Journal*, December 6, 1925, "and when a little shanty town sprung up at the foot of the West Mound it was voted in the language of the times to call it 'damned Pokerville.'" "Fortunes were won and lost every night," remarked Fred Holmes in the *State Journal*, February 26, 1922: "liquor flowed freely, and bloodshed and killings were not unknown."

Twenty years later the railroad came through (on what is now the Military Ridge Recreational Trail), but its depot was located a mile east of Pokerville, where the village of Blue Mounds is today. This doomed the little hamlet to oblivion, and Pokerville's residents scattered around the country. In 1871 three Adams brothers of Pokerville moved to Colorado, where two of them took turns serving as governor and the third became a U.S. senator. Back in Wisconsin, meanwhile, their hometown gradually collapsed and composted, until by 1925 it was hardly visible amid the farm fields.

# "The Woods Are Full of Ghosts!"

The Nashotah Theological Seminary in Waukesha County was founded by Reverend James Lloyd Breck and three companions in 1842 as a center for the Episcopal Church in Wisconsin Territory, and it received its official charter from the government in 1847. Breck went on to found many churches and other religious institutions across the upper Midwest before his death in California in 1876. After a few years, Episcopal leaders in Wisconsin asked that his body be brought back to Nashotah, and that's when the trouble occurred. This account comes from a *New York Times* reporter, who claimed, on December 7, 1902, only to "relate the tale as the Nashotah people tell it, and the reader can draw his own conclusions."

*After its arrival the casket containing the body of Dr. Breck lay for a time on the ground floor of one of the buildings, and watchers sat with it. On the night before the reburial, the watchers were the Rev. Charles P. Dorset, for fifteen years rector of St. James, in Chicago, now [1902] of the Diocese of Texas, and Dr. Wilson, now of Chicago. Along in the hours near morning Wilson stepped out for a breath of fresh air, but in a moment came rushing back, with the exclamation, "Dorset, Dorset, the woods are full of ghosts!"*

*Both clergymen went out. In every direction through the trees they saw figures darting hither and thither in a wild and fitful dance. The clergymen approached, but the figures drew back before them, forming to left and right of them, and it was impossible to get within close range. In the morning, when the casket was lifted, the floor beneath was found to have been blackened by fire, and a hole was actually burned through to the space beneath.*

As if a forest alive with ghosts and a hole burned through the floor were not enough, the situation grew weirder as the reburial of Breck's body approached:

*At night the Faculty of the institution sat in the office of Dr. Gardiner, the President, discussing the strange events that perplexed them. Suddenly their discussions were abruptly terminated by a startling and tremendous racket just outside the door, a clattering and whacking that was deafening. Dr. Gardiner threw open the door. Not a soul in the hall. He returned to his room, but hardly had he sat down when the noises began again. Again a sudden dash into the hall failed to reveal any one. Nor did a search of the building reveal that outside the Faculty a living being was in it. A third time the noises began, and this time Dr. Gardiner spoke into the hall: "If you are gentlemen, be still." The noise stopped.*

The interment of the remains proceeded without incident, probably to the collective relief of Nashotah staff who had witnessed the previous days' events. But "after the reburial of Dr. Breck, a photograph was taken of the cemetery. One of the students was the photographer. In the foreground of the picture can be seen two graves, just as they appear in the cemetery. But at the foot of each grave stands something no visitor has ever seen, and for the peace of his mind it is hoped never will see."

*At the foot of one grave stands the Rev. Dr. Cole, a former President of the seminary, in full canonicals [Reverend Azel D. Cole, who had died in 1885]. At the foot of the other grave stands the counterfeit presentment of its occupant, a woman who in life was a benefactress of the school.*

*When these startling things appeared at the time the photograph was developed, the seminary authorities decided that possibly some well-timed conjunction of sunlight and foliage was the cause of the images; that they had no real existence—were only shadows. So they had the picture thrown on a screen by a stereopticon. But the figures came out more plainly—so plainly that there was no denying that they were the well-remembered features of Dr. Cole and the seminary's benefactress.*

*Still, there were those who suspected the photographer of a trick and charged him with it. He denied the charge and offered this unassailable plea of innocence: there was no such thing as a photograph of Dr. Cole in existence and nobody had ever heard of one.*

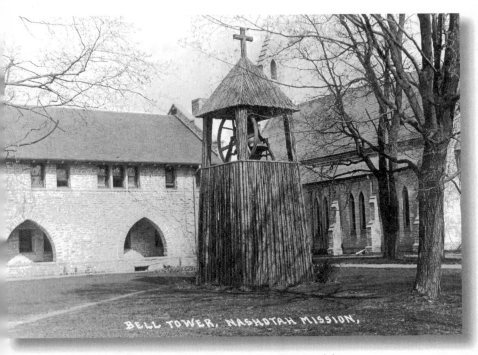

BELL TOWER, NASHOTAH MISSION,

*Nashotah Mission, site of ghostly apparitions.*

WHi Image ID 41562

183

# Index

## The Author

Joel Heiman

*Erika Janik* grew up in Redmond, Washington, but now knows more about Wisconsin history than she ever thought possible. She has master's degrees in American history and journalism from the University of Wisconsin–Madison and has written many essays and articles on Wisconsin history for the Wisconsin Historical Society online collections and as editor of the Society's membership newsletter. She coordinated the Society's digital collection "Turning Points in Wisconsin History," wrote dozens of topical essays on state history as well as a short history of the state, composed encyclopedic dictionary entries on Wisconsin, and continues to provide regular feature stories for the Society homepage. Her work has appeared in *Wisconsin Trails* magazine, *On Wisconsin, Renewing the Countryside, Isthmus, Wisconsin Magazine of History,* and the *Wisconsin State Journal.*